McDougal Littell
The
AMERICANS

Workbook

McDougal Littell
A HOUGHTON MIFFLIN COMPANY

Evanston, Illinois • Boston • Dallas

gift

Table of Contents

How to Use The Americans Workbook

Each page in *The Americans Workbook* guides you through your reading of one section in *The Americans*. Your notes and responses in this book can help you participate in classroom discussions. The notes can also become study aids as you prepare for quizzes, tests, or longer projects.

Each **Guided Reading** page allows you to preview a section, to take notes in graphic organizers, and to jot down answers to questions, interacting with history as you read. Each page ends with a question or extended writing activity asking you to use **key terms and names** from the section.

Name _____   Date _____

A. As you read about the development of Native American cultures, fill out the chart below by writing notes that describe the achievements of those cultures.

	Achievements
1. The Olmec	
2. The Maya, Aztec, and Inca	
3. The Hohokam and Anasazi	
4. The Adena, Hopewell, and Mississippian	

B. What was the Beringia Land Bridge and what was its importance in the settlement of the Americas?

_____

_____

C. On the back of this paper, record the dates of the rise and decline (if possible) as well as the locations of each of the following cultures:

Olmec   Maya   Aztec   Inca   Hohokam   Anasazi

Name _____ Date _____

GUIDED READING *Native American Societies Around 1492*

Section 2

A. As you read about early Native American cultures, write notes about some
common patterns of trade, views of land use, religious beliefs, and social values
that they all shared.

1. Trading networks	2. Land use
3. Religious beliefs	4. Social organization

B. On the back of this paper, note something significant you learned about each of the
following Native American groups:

Kashaya Pomo   **Kwakiutl**   **Pueblo**   **Iroquois**

Name _____ Date _____

CHAPTER
1
Section 3

GUIDED READING *West African Societies Around 1492*

A. As you read about societies in West Africa, fill out this cause-and-effect chart.

Cause
Early contacts between West African and Portuguese traders.

Effects on West Africa
1.

Effects on the Americas
2.

B. Summarize some of the following important characteristics of West African societies around 1492.

1. Family and government
2. Religion
3. Work
4. Slave labor

C. On the back of this paper, identify or explain each of the following:

savanna   Islam   plantation   Songhai
Benin   Kongo   lineage

Name _____ Date _____

GUIDED READING *European Societies Around 1492*

A. As you read this section, fill out the chart below by writing answers in the appropriate boxes.

	How did each event or trend encourage European exploration?
1. The Crusades	
2. The growth of commerce	
3. The growth of population	
4. The rise of nations	
5. The Renaissance	
6. The improvement in sailing technology	

B. On the back of this paper, define or explain each of the following:

Prince Henry   **hierarchy**   **nuclear family**   **Reformation**

Name _____ Date _____

CHAPTER 1

Section 5

GUIDED READING *Transatlantic Encounters*

A. As you read, take notes about Columbus's explorations.

1. Columbus failed to meet the primary goal of his first voyage (to find a western route to Asia), but he succeeded in meeting several other important goals. What were those goals?
2. What reasons do you think motivated certain groups of Spaniards to join Columbus on his later voyages to the Americas?

B. In the chart below, summarize the effects that European exploration and colonization of the Americas had on the following three regions of the world and their inhabitants.

1. The Americas and Native Americans
2. Africa and its peoples
3. Europe and its peoples

C. On the back of this paper, answer the following questions:

1. Who were the **Taino,** and what does that name mean?

2. What agreement was reached in the **Treaty of Tordesillas?**

3. Define the **Columbian Exchange** and give several specific examples of its effects.

Name _____ Date _____

A. As you read this section, fill out the chart below to help you better understand the motivations and methods behind the conquests of the conquistadores.

The Spanish Conquest of Central and North America

Motivations	Methods
1. What motivated Spain's conquest?	2. How were the Spanish able to succeed?

Spanish Rule of New Spain and New Mexico

Motivations	Methods
3. Why did Spain establish these colonies?	4. How did Spain control these colonies?

Resistance to Spanish Rule in New Mexico

Motivations	Results
5. Why did the Pueblos rebel against Spain?	6. What resulted from Popé's rebellion?

B. On the back of this paper, identify or define each of the following:

conquistadores	**Hernando Cortés**	**mestizo**	*encomienda*
Juan Ponce de León	*congregaciones*	**Popé**	

CHAPTER
2
Section 2

GUIDED READING *An English Settlement at Jamestown*

A. As you read this section, fill out the chart below to help you better understand the motivations and methods behind the conquests of the conquistadores.

1. **Who?** Who were the settlers? Who were their leaders? Who were their neighbors?	
2. **What?** What type of colony was Jamestown at first? What did it later become?	
3. **When?** When was Jamestown settled? When was the "starving time"?	
4. **Why?** Why did the settlers go to Jamestown? Why did others support them? Why didn't the settlers get along with their neighbors? Why did Jamestown nearly fail?	
5. **Where?** Where was Jamestown?	
6. **How?** How was Jamestown saved from failure?	

B. On the back of this paper, identify or define each of the following:

conquistadores	**Hernando Cortés**	**mestizo**	*encomienda*
Juan Ponce de León	*congregaciones*	**Popé**	

Name _____ Date _____

GUIDED READING *Puritan New England*

A. As you read this section, fill out the chart below by writing notes that summarize the causes and results of the conflicts.

	CAUSES OF THE CONFLICT	RESULTS OF THE CONFLICT
1. Puritans *vs.* the Church of England		
2. Puritan leaders *vs.* Roger Williams		
3. Puritan leaders *vs.* Anne Hutchinson		
4. The Pequot War		
5. King Philip's War		

B. On the back of this paper, create a word web for each of the following:

John Winthrop   **Separatist**

Name _____ Date _____

Settlement of the Middle Colonies

As you read about New Netherland and Pennsylvania, fill out the chart below by writing notes that describe aspects of each colony.

NEW NETHERLAND			
1. Population	2. Economy	3. Relations with Native Americans	4. Relations with England

PENNSYLVANIA			
5. Proprietor	6. Population	7. Religion	8. Relations with Native Americans

Name _____ Date _____

GUIDED READING *England and Its Colonies*

A. As you read this section, answer the questions below to help you understand causes and effects. There can be one or several answers to each question.

The Navigation Acts

CAUSE
1. Why did Parliament pass the Navigation Acts?

EFFECTS
2. How did these acts benefit England?
3. How did the acts benefit the colonies?
4. How did the acts hurt the colonies?

The Glorious Revolution

CAUSE
5. Why did the Glorious Revolution occur?

EFFECTS
6. How did this revolution affect England?
7. How did it affect the colonies?

B. On the back of this paper, explain the relationship in each of the following pairs:

balance of trade—mercantilism   **salutary neglect—mercantilism**
Dominion of New England—Sir Edmund Adros

GUIDED READING *The Agricultural South*

A. As you read this section, fill out the chart below by noting what a typical member of each group would likely do in his or her daily life.

1. Plantation Owners

2. Lower-Class White Women

3. Indentured Servants

4. African Slaves

B. On the back of this paper, explain or identify each of the following:

cash crop   **triangular trade**   **middle passage**   **Stono Rebellion**

Name _____ Date _____

CHAPTER
3
Section 3

GUIDED READING *The Commercial North*

A. As you read this section, fill out the chart below with some different characteristics of the Northern and Southern colonies.

Northern Colonies	Southern Colonies

B. Fill out this chart by comparing the Enlightenment and the Great Awakening.

	The Enlightenment	The Great Awakening
1. What kind of movement was it (intellectual, social, political, religious)?		
2. Who were its key figures in the colonies?		
3. What ideas did it stress?		
4. What did it encourage people to do?		

Name _____   Date _____

CHAPTER 3

Section 4

GUIDED READING *The French and Indian War*

A. Fill out the charts below as you read about the French and Indian War (1754–1763).

Motivations		
1. Why did France and Britain fight in the war?	2. Why did the British colonies fight?	3. Why did Native Americans fight?

Winners and Losers	
4. What did Britain gain as a result of the war?	5. What did Britain lose?
6. What did the colonies gain as a result of the war?	7. What did the colonies lose?
8. What did France lose as a result of the war?	9. What did the war cost Native Americans?

B. On the back of this paper, define or describe each of the following:

George Washington   William Pitt   Pontiac

George Grenville   Sugar Act   Proclamation of 1763

Name _____ Date _____

GUIDED READING *The Stirrings of Rebellion*

A. As you read this section, trace the following sequence of events.

1a. The British Parliament passed the Stamp Act (1765) in order to . . .	b. Colonists responded to the act by . . .	c. Britain responded to the colonists by . . .
2a. The British Parliament passed the Townshend Act (1767) in order to . . .	b. Colonists responded to the act by . . .	c. Britain responded to the colonists by . . .
3a. The British Parliament passed the Tea Act (1773) in order to . . .	b. Colonists responded to the act by . . .	c. Britain responded to the colonists by . . .
4a. The British Parliament passed the Intolerable Acts (1774) in order to . . .	b. Colonists responded to the act by . . .	c. Britain responded to the colonists by . . .

B. On the back of this paper, identify or explain each of the following:

Samuel Adams	**Boston Massacre**	**committees of correspondence**
Boston Tea Party	**King George III**	**martial law**

Name _____ Date _____

A. As you read this section, trace the following sequence of events.

1774 Sept.	The first Continental Congress convenes. It agrees to meet again if problems with Britain continue.	1. What does the Continental Congress do to bring about peace?
1775 Apr.	Clashes between British soldiers and American minutemen at Lexington and Concord result in the loss of life.	
May	Since problems with the British intensify, the Second Continental Congress meets.	2. What does the Continental Congress do to prepare for war?
Fall & Winter	Fighting between the British and the colonists increases.	3. What are the main ideas of *Common Sense?*
		4. What is the purpose of a formal declaration of independence?
1776 Jan.	Thomas Paine publishes his *Common Sense* pamphlet.	
July	With the increase of fighting between Britain and the colonies, the Continental Congress adopts the Declaration of Independence.	5. What are the main ideas of the Declaration of Independence?

B. On the back of this paper, identify or explain each of the following:

Samuel Adams   **Boston Massacre**   **committees of correspondence**

Name _____ Date _____

A. As you read this section, write answers to the questions about each of the Revolutionary War battles listed below.

	Who won?	Why did they win?	What were the important results?
1. New York			
2. Trenton			
3. Philadelphia			
4. Saratoga			

B. Summarize the difficulties faced by each group of Patriots during the Revolutionary War?

Patriots	What were some of the hardships they faced?
1. Soldiers	
2. Members of Congress	
3. Civilians	

C. On the back of this paper, identify or define each of the following:

Valley Forge   **inflation**   **profiteering**

CHAPTER
4
Section 4

GUIDED READING *Winning the War*

A. As you read this section, trace the following sequence of events.

1. Friedrich von Steuben	2. Marquis de Lafayette
3. The Battle of Yorktown	4. The signing of the Treaty of Paris

B. On the back of this paper, identify or explain each of the following:

Samuel Adams   **Boston Massacre**   **committees of correspondence**
Boston Tea Party   **King George III**   **martial law**

Name _____ Date _____

GUIDED READING *Experimenting with*
Confederation

A. As you read, take notes that summarize how delegates to the Continental Congress
answered three main questions about the new federal government.

1. Representation: By population or by state?	2. Supreme power: Can it be divided?	3. Western lands: Who gets them?

B. As you read this section, make notes that answer the questions below.

1. What was the new nation's major financial problem? _____

_____

2. Why was the national government unable to solve its financial problems? _____

_____

3. Why didn't Congress amend the Articles so it could impose a tariff? _____

_____

_____

4. Why do you suppose the central government under the Articles of Confederation was given such

limited powers? _____

_____

_____

_____

C. On the back of this paper, define **republic, republicanism,** and **confederation.**
Then briefly explain each of the following:

Land Ordinance of 1785   **Northwest Ordinance of 1787**

Name _____ Date _____

CHAPTER 5

Section 2

GUIDED READING *Drafting the Constitution*

A. As you read how our Constitution was developed, take notes summarizing issues in the chart below.

1. The Virginia Plan proposed a Congress composed of:	2. The New Jersey Plan called for a Congress consisting of:

↓

3. The Virginia Plan proposed that representation in Congress be based on: Other large states agreed.	4. The New Jersey Plan proposed that congressional representation be based on: Other small states agreed.

5. How did the Great Compromise resolve this conflict?

↓

6. Northern states felt that representation in Congress should be based on the number of:	7. Southern states felt that representation should be based on the number of:

8. How did the Three-Fifths Compromise resolve this conflict?

B. On the back of this paper, identify or explain each of the following:

Shays's Rebellion   Roger Sherman   legislative branch   judicial branch

James Madison   checks and balances   executive branch   electoral college

Name _____ Date _____

A. As you read this section, fill out the chart below with information about the people and ideas involved in the debate over the ratification of the Constitution.

1. Who were the most important Federalists? Identify individuals and groups.	2. Who were the most important Antifederalists? Identify individuals and groups.
3. What were Federalist reasons for supporting ratification?	4. What were Antifederalist reasons for opposing ratification?

B. Which rights do each of the following constitutional amendments in the Bill of Rights protect?

1. First Amendment	2. Fourth Amendment

C. On the back of this paper, explain the relationship between the **Federalist Papers** and the **ratification** of the U.S. Constitution.

Name _____ Date _____

GUIDED READING *Preamble and Article 1*

As you read the Preamble and Article 1 of the Constitution, answer the questions below. Circle **Yes** or **No** for each question and provide the location of the information that supports your answer. All information is in Article 1, so you need to supply only the section and clause information. Section 4, Clause 2 would be written 4.2.

Yes (No)

Example: Do states have varying numbers of Senators? _____ Location   **3.1**

1. Lois Deevers, a Texan for two years, is 26 years old and has been a U.S. citizen for ten years. Could she serve as a congresswoman from Texas? _____   Yes   No   Location _____

2. Ky Pham is 32 years old and became a U.S. citizen at the age of 24. Could he serve as a senator from Maine, where he has lived his entire life? _____   Yes · No   Location _____

3. If the Senate votes 49 to 49 on a bill, does the President of the Senate cast the tie-breaking vote? _____   Yes   No   Location _____

4. Can a senator be sued for slander because of things he or she said in a speech on the floor of the Senate? _____   Yes   No   Location _____

5. If Congress creates a new government agency, can a senator or representative resign from office to become the head of that agency? _____   Yes   No   Location _____

6. Can the Senate expel one of its members? _____   Yes   No   Location _____

7. If the House unanimously votes to override a presidential veto, and the Senate votes to override by a vote of 64 to 34, does the bill become law? _____   Yes   No   Location _____

8. Can Congress pass an *ex post facto* law if both houses favor it by a two-thirds majority? _____   Yes   No   Location _____

9. Can a state impose an import tax on goods entering from another state? _____   Yes   No   Location _____

10. Could a bill pass the Senate by a vote of 26 to 27? _____   Yes   No   Location _____

11. If a bill is sent to the president one week before Congress adjourns, and the president neither signs it nor returns it, does it become law? _____   Yes   No   Location _____

12. Can a state legally engage in war with a foreign nation if the state is invaded by troops of that nation? _____   Yes   No   Location _____

Name _____ Date _____

GUIDED READING *Articles 2 and 3*

As you read Articles 2 and 3, answer each of the following questions by writing **Yes** or **No** on the blank line. Each question is specifically answered by the Constitution.

Article 2

_____ 1. Is the length of a president's term set by the Constitution?

_____ 2. Does the number of electors that each state has in the Electoral College vary from state to state?

_____ 3. Must national elections be held in November?

_____ 4. Can a 30-year-old, natural-born citizen hold the office of president?

_____ 5. Can an 80-year-old person who became a U.S. citizen at the age of 21 hold the office of president?

_____ 6. Does a president's salary always remain the same while in office?

_____ 7. Must someone elected to the presidency take an oath before taking office?

_____ 8. Can the president pardon someone convicted of treason?

_____ 9. Must the president report to Congress about how the nation is doing?

_____ 10. Can a president convicted of bribery remain in office?

Article 3

_____ 11. Can a president dismiss a member of the Supreme Court and replace him or her with someone more in agreement with the president?

_____ 12. Can the salary paid to a federal judge be lowered while that judge remains in office?

_____ 13. Must a case in which a resident of Nebraska sues a citizen of Louisiana be heard in a federal court?

_____ 14. Can someone who publicly urges others to overthrow the federal government be convicted of treason for that position?

_____ 15. Can a person who gives secret information about U.S. military plans to a foreign government be convicted of treason?

_____ 16. Can a person who denies having committed treason be convicted on the testimony of a single person who witnessed the treasonous act?

GUIDED READING *Articles 4–7*

As you read Articles 4-7, answer the following questions and note the article (with section and clause, when necessary) that is the source for the relevant information. Article 4, Section 3, Clause 2 would be written 4.3.2.

Example: Could Utah refuse to allow a U.S. citizen from Ohio to buy a home in Utah? (Yes) No Location 4.2

Article 4

1. Must one state honor the ruling of a state court in another state? .... Yes No
   Location _____

2. If a woman commits a crime in Kentucky and is captured in New York, can New York refuse to return her to Kentucky? .... Yes No
   Location _____

3. Would it be possible for North and South Dakota to become one state if both state legislatures, and Congress, approved of such a merger? .... Yes No
   Location _____

4. Can one state establish a dictatorship within that state as long as it does not interfere with the lives of citizens in other states? .... Yes No
   Location _____

Article 5

5. What institution decides when an amendment to the Constitution should be proposed and considered? .... Answer _____
   Location _____

6. How many states must approve an amendment for it to take effect? .... Answer _____
   Location _____

Article 6

7. Can one state enforce a law within its own borders that conflicts with a national law? .... Yes No
   Location _____

8. If a man refused to support the Constitution, could he serve as a member of his state's legislature? .... Yes No
   Location _____

9. Can an atheist be denied the right to hold federal office? .... Yes No
   Location _____

Article 7

10. How many states had to ratify the Constitution for it to become the law of the land? .... Answer _____
    Location _____

11. In what year was the Constitution signed by delegates to the Constitutional Convention? .... Answer _____
    Location _____

Name _____ Date _____

GUIDED READING *The Amendments*

As you read the amendments to the Constitution, circle the correct choice from each parenthetical pair of choices in the summary below.

Amendment 1   establishes the people's right to (vote/criticize the government).
Amendment 2   maintains that states have the right to have (armed militias/legislatures).
Amendment 3   protects people from being forced to (serve as/house) soldiers in peacetime.
Amendment 4   requires police to provide a (good reason/written accusation) to obtain a search warrant.
Amendment 5   guarantees that the government cannot take private property for its own use without (the owner's agreement/fair payment).
Amendment 6   protects the rights of (crime victims/people accused of crimes).
Amendment 7   requires that most people accused of civil crimes be given a (jury/speedy) trial.
Amendment 8   says that bails, fines, and punishments for crimes cannot be (delayed/unfair or cruel).
Amendment 9   states that people's rights (are/are not) limited to those listed in the Constitution.
Amendment 10   says that government powers not mentioned in the Constitution belong to (the states or the people/the House of Representatives).
Amendment 11   prohibits a citizen of one state from suing another (state/citizen) in a federal court.
Amendment 12   requires that electors for president and vice-president clearly identify (the party each candidate belongs to/the person they choose for each office).
Amendment 13   forbids slavery in the (South/United States).
Amendment 14   requires that states give all people (the right to vote/equal protection under the law).
Amendment 15   prohibits denying voting rights because of (sex/race).
Amendment 16   establishes Congress's right to pass (an income/a sales) tax.
Amendment 17   changes the way in which (the president/U.S. senators) are elected.
Amendment 18   establishes (prohibition/civil rights).
Amendment 19   prohibits denying the right to vote based on (age/sex).
Amendment 20   (shortens/lengthens) the time between elections and taking office.
Amendment 21   repeals Amendment (17/18).
Amendment 22   limits the (years/number) of presidential terms.
Amendment 23   gives residents of Washington, D.C., the right to vote in (presidential/local) elections.
Amendment 24   forbids a tax on (voting/property).
Amendment 25   establishes when and how the (Speaker of the House/vice-president) can take over presidential powers.
Amendment 26   extends suffrage to (residents/citizens) who are 18 years of age.
Amendment 27   deals with pay raises for (members of Congress/the president).

Name _____ Date _____

A. Fill out the chart below, taking notes about Washington's two terms as president.

Government Organization	
1. What did the Judiciary Act of 1789 establish?	2. What departments did Washington create and whom did he appoint to head them?

Philosophies of Government	
3. How did Jefferson feel about political power and the common people?	4. How did Hamilton feel about political power and the common people?
5. Why did Jefferson and Madison oppose the national bank?	6. Why did Hamilton support the national bank?

Party Politics	
7. To which party did Jefferson belong?	8. To which party did Hamilton belong?
9. Why did Washington distrust the two-party system?	

B. On the back of this paper, briefly define each of the following:

    cabinet   **protective tariff**   **excise tax**   **Republicans**

Name _____ Date _____

CHAPTER
6
Section 2

GUIDED READING *Foreign Affairs*
Trouble the Nation

A. As you read about the U.S. government's first experiences with foreign affairs, take
notes to answer questions about events appearing on the time line.

1793	Declaration of neutrality	→	1. What were the reasons for issuing this declaration?
1794	Battle of Fallen Timbers	→	2. What resulted from this U.S. victory?
	Jay's Treaty	→	3. What did Britain and the United States agree to?
1795	Pinckney's Treaty	→	4. What did Spain and the United States agree to?
1796	Adams elected president	→	5. What problems did this election underscore?
	XYZ Affair	→	6. What effect did the affair have on U.S.-French relations?
1798	Alien and Sedition Acts	→	7. What measures were contained in these acts?
	Virginia and Kentucky Resolutions	→	8. What did these resolutions declare?

B. On the back of this paper, identify or explain each of the following:

    Edmond Genêt   **Little Turtle**   **John Jay**   **sectionalism**

Name _____ Date _____

A. As you read about Jefferson's presidency, write answers to the questions below.

Key Trends in Jefferson's Administration
1. How did Jefferson simplify the federal government?
2. How did Jefferson's presidency help bring about Southern dominance in federal politics?
3. How did the Federalists lose power during the Jefferson administration?

Key Events in the Jefferson Administration
4. What was the long-term importance of the Supreme Court's decision in *Marbury* v. *Madison?*
5. How did the Louisiana Purchase affect the United States and its government?
6. Who led the exploration of the Louisiana Territory?

B. On the back of this paper, explain how each of the following are related:

    Judiciary Act of 1801   **midnight judges**   **John Marshall**   **judicial review**

C. On the back of this paper, identify each of the following:

    Aaron Burr   **Daniel Boone**   **Sacajawea**

Name _____ Date _____

CHAPTER
6
Section 4

GUIDED READING *The War of 1812*

A. Write notes describing what each president did to deal with a stated problem. Then, write notes to explain why the president's response succeeded, failed, or had mixed results in solving the problem.

1. President Thomas Jefferson

Problem	Response
War between Great Britain and France resulted in the seizure of American ships and, at times, the impressment of Americans into the British navy.	

Reasons for the success or failure of Jefferson's response:

2. President James Madison

Problem	Response
Great Britain seized American ships and sailors and was thought to have encouraged Native American attacks on American settlers.	

Reasons for the success or failure of Madison's response:

B. On the back of this paper, explain or identify each of the following:

| blockade | embargo | war hawks | William Henry Harrison |
| Tecumseh | Andrew Jackson | Treaty of Ghent | armistice |

Name _____ Date _____

CHAPTER 7
Section 1

GUIDED READING *Regional Economies*
Create Differences

A. As you read about regional issues in early U.S. history, fill out the chart by writing
answers to the questions below.

The Industrial Revolution takes hold in the United States.

Regional Economy	Regional Agriculture
1. What was the North's economy based on?	2. What were the main elements of the North's agricultural system?
3. What was the South's economy based on?	4. What were the main elements of the South's agricultural system?

Henry Clay champions the American System.

5. What were the main goals of the American System?		
6. How was each of the following intended to help the United States achieve those goals?		
Tariff of 1816	The Second Bank of the United States	Internal improvements

B. On the back of this paper, explain how the terms and names in each of the
following sets are related.

  1. Eli Whitney—interchangeable parts—mass production
  2. National Road—Erie Canal

Balancing Nationalism and Sectionalism 29

Name _____ Date _____

CHAPTER
7
Section 2

GUIDED READING *Nationalism at Center Stage*

A. As you read about the rise of national feeling in the U.S., answer questions about the measures and policies in the chart below.

	What ideas did the measure contain?	How did it promote nationalism?
1. *Gibbons* v. *Ogden* decision		
2. The Adams-Onis Treaty		
3. The Monroe Doctrine		
4. The Missouri Compromise		

B. On the back of this paper, summarize what you know about **John Quincy Adams** and **Jim Beckwourth.**

Name _____ Date _____

A. As you read about the Jacksonian era, write answers to the questions about events that appear on the time line.

1827	By this point, the Cherokee have established themselves as a nation. →	**1. Who were the "five civilized tribes"?**
1830	Congress passes the Indian Removal Act. Jackson forces the Choctaw from their lands. →	**2. What did the act call for, and why did Andrew Jackson support it?**
1831	Jackson forces the Sauk and Fox from their lands.	
1832	Jackson forces the Chickasaw from their lands.	
	The Supreme Court rules on *Worcester* v. *Georgia*. →	**3. What did the court decide in the case?**
1835	The Cherokee begin leaving Georgia. →	**4. What was Jackson's response to the court ruling?**
1838	President Van Buren orders the forced removal of all Cherokee from Georgia. →	**5. Why is this forced removal referred to as the Trail of Tears?**

B. On the back of this paper, identify or explain each of the following:

Democratic-Republican Party   **spoils system**

GUIDED READING *Jackson, States' Rights, and the National Bank*

CHAPTER 7

Section 4

A. As you read, fill out the chart with details about two major controversies.

Nullification Conflict	
1. Key Players:	2. Key Events:
3. Causes:	4. Results:

Bank of the United States Conflict	
5. Key Players:	6. Key Events:
7. Causes:	8. Results:

B. On the back of this paper, note something important about each of the following:

  Panic of 1837   **Martin Van Buren**   **William Henry Harrison**   **John Tyler**

Name _____ Date _____

CHAPTER 8
Section 1

GUIDED READING *Religion Sparks Reform*

A. As you read about reform movements, answer the questions below.

Late 1700s: New religious and philosophical movements emerge during the Second Great Awakening.

What ideas and practices did each of the following promote?
1. Revivalism
2. Unitarian movement
3. African Methodist Episcopal church
4. Transcendentalism

Mid-1800s: By this time, Americans from numerous religious and philosophical movements joined together to fight the social ills that were troubling the nation.

5. What did the movement to reform education accomplish?
6. What were the accomplishments of the movement to reform asylums and prisons?
7. What were the purposes of utopian communities?

B. On the back of this paper, briefly describe the relationship of each of the following to the reform movements of the 1880s.

Charles G. Finney	Ralph Waldo Emerson	Henry David Thoreau
Dorothea Dix	Brook Farm	

Name _____ Date _____

GUIDED READING *Slavery and Abolition*

A. As you read, fill out the chart below.

By the 1820s, slavery had once again become a hotly debated issue, even among those who opposed it.

Describe the plan of action for the abolition of slavery favored by each of the following abolitionists.		
1. William Lloyd Garrison	2. David Walker	3. Frederick Douglass

By the 1820s, most African Americans living in America had been born here. Their experiences varied widely, depending on where they lived and whether they were free.

Describe the lives of people in each of the following groups of African Americans.		
4. Rural slaves	5. Urban slaves	6. Free blacks

In 1831, Nat Turner led slaves in a bloody rebellion. A frightened and outraged South cracked down on African Americans, both slave and free.

7. What new restrictions were placed on African Americans?	8. What new arguments were made to support slavery?	9. What was done in Congress to prevent debate on slavery?

B. On the back of this paper, briefly explain each of the following:

emancipation   **antebellum**   **gag rule**

Name _____ Date _____

CHAPTER

8

Section 3

GUIDED READING *Women and Reform*

A. As you read, fill out responses below, summarizing the early developments and identifying the leaders of the women's rights movement.

> **Discriminated against at the 1840 World's Anti-Slavery Convention, Elizabeth Cady Stanton and Lucretia Mott vowed "to hold a convention . . . and form a society to advocate the rights of women."**

1. In what ways were women's options limited in the early 19th century?

> **Despite such limitations, women participated in all the important reform movements of the 19th century.**

Movement	Key Women Leaders	Efforts Made on Behalf of the Movement
2. Abolitionism		
3. Temperance		
4. Women's education		
5. Health reform for women		
6. Women's rights		

B. On the back of this paper, briefly identify or describe each of the following:

cult of domesticity   **Sojourner Truth**   **Seneca Falls convention**

Name _____ Date _____

A. As you read about changes in the workplace, supply the missing causes or effects.

Causes	Effects
1.	The cottage industry system declines and dies.
The Industrial Revolution sparks the rapid spread of factory production	2.
The Industrial Revolution brings about the use of production processes dependent on new machines and interchangeable parts.	3.
4.	Young farm girls and women flock to Lowell and other mill towns.
5.	Workers strike at Lowell in 1834 and 1836.
The company threatens to recruit local women to fill strikers' jobs; strikers are criticized by the local press and clergy; strike leaders are fired.	6.
7.	Male artisans and unskilled workers also strike in the 1830s and 1840s.
Unskilled workers become easily replaceable by immigrants eager for work.	8.
Poor wages; poor working conditions; long workdays; ease of breaking strikes all point to the need for unity among laborers.	9.
The Supreme Court hands down its decision in *Commonwealth* v. *Hunt.*	10.

B. On the back of this paper, briefly describe the relationship among the following.

master   **journeyman**   **apprentice**t

Name _____ Date _____

CHAPTER 9
Section 1

GUIDED READING *The Market Revolution*

A. As you read about the formation of the national market economy, fill out the charts.

How did these inventions help expand the national market economy?	
1. Sewing machine (and improvements)	
2. Telegraph	
3. Steamboat	
4. Railroad	
5. Steel plow	
6. Mechanical reaper	

How did these innovations promote the new market economy?	
7. Entrepreneurial activity	
8. Canals	
9. National Road	
10. Industrialization	

B. On the back of this paper, briefly explain how the people or innovations in each set are related:

    1. **specialization—John Deere—Cyrus McCormick**
    2. **market revolution—capitalism—Samuel F. B. Morse**

Name _____ Date _____

A. As you read about expansion to areas of the West, fill out the charts.

Despite the hardships of the journey and the difficult living conditions at journey's end, the West drew increasing numbers of Americans during the mid-19th century.

	New Mexico	Oregon	Utah
1. Who went?			
2. Why did they go?			
3. How did they get there?			
4. What did they find when they got there?			

On the trip west, Americans passed through or even settled on Native American lands. Native Americans and the U.S. government responded in various ways.

5. The Black Hawk War	6. The Fort Laramie Treaty
Causes:	Causes:
Results:	Results:

B. On the back of this paper, briefly explain the relationship among the following:

Joseph Smith—Brigham Young—Mormons

C. On the back of this paper, define the following:

manifest destiny   middle ground   "Fifty-four Forty or Fight!"

Name _____ Date _____

CHAPTER
9
Section 3

GUIDED READING *Expansion in Texas*

A. As you read this section, answer questions about the time line.

1821	**Mexico offers land grants to anyone bringing settlers to Texas.**
1823	
1824	

1. Why did Mexico want Americans to settle in Texas?

2. Why did Americans want to settle in Texas?

▼

3. What brought American settlers into conflict with the Mexican government?

▼

1835	**The Texas Revolution is led by Texans eager to gain independence from Mexico.**

4. What happened at the Alamo?

▼

1836	**The Republic of Texas is founded.**
1838	**Sam Houston invites the United States to annex the new republic.**

5. Why was the United States at first reluctant to annex Texas?

1845	**Texas becomes the twenty-eighth state of the Union.**

B. On the back of this paper, explain why **Stephen F. Austin** and **Antonio López de Santa Anna** were major historical figures.

CHAPTER
9
Section 4

GUIDED READING *The War with Mexico*

A. As you read about the war with Mexico, fill in the blanks in the following summary. You may need to abbreviate.

Mexico was angered when Texas was annexed—and became a state—in 1845. In addition, Mexico and the United States disagreed about the location of Texas's

(1) _____. U.S. President (2) _____

sent Slidell to Mexico with an unsuccessful offer to purchase disputed land in Texas

and the Mexican-owned territories of (3) _____ and California.

When (4) _____'s troops blockaded the (5) _____,

Mexico viewed the action as an invasion and attacked the U.S. soldiers near Matamoros.

In response, President Polk successfully urged Congress to declare war. Polk then

ordered General Kearny to capture (6) _____, which was

accomplished without bloodshed. In the meantime, American settlers in (7) _____

led by John C. Fremont overthrew the Mexican government in the town of Sonoma

and established an independent nation that they called the (8) _____.

General (9) _____ arrived and joined forces with the U.S.

Navy to complete the conquest of (10) _____.

The war with Mexico was also going on in the territory of (11) _____

and in Mexico. In September 1846, General (12) _____'s troops

captured the city of Monterrey. (13) _____ did not honor

an agreement made with Polk to end the war and led troops in a battle at Buena Vista,

which they lost. In the meantime, General Scott moved toward (14) _____,

and captured the capital.

The signing of the Treaty of (15) _____ ended the war.

As a result, the United States gained vast amounts of land. More was added when

President (16) _____ authorized the (17) _____

in 1853. These two events, together, set the present-day borders of the lower 48 states.

B. On the back of this paper, describe the relationship between the **Forty-niners** and the **gold rush.**

Name _____ Date _____

A. The time line below reviews important events related to the issue of slavery. As you read about the political effects of this issue, take notes summarizing the terms of the Compromise of 1850 and the part played by several key players in developing it.

1787	The Three-Fifths Compromise attempts to settle issues of slavery and representation in the Northwest Ordinance. Congress bans slavery in territories north of the Ohio River.
1820	The Missouri Compromise attempts to balance the power of North and South by admitting Maine as a free state and Missouri as a slave state.
1845	Texas is admitted to the Union as a slave state.
1848	The war with Mexico comes to an end, and Americans ask themselves whether territories won in the war should be open to slavery.
1849	California's application for statehood forces the nation to deal with the issue of the expansion of slavery.
1850	Compromise of 1850.

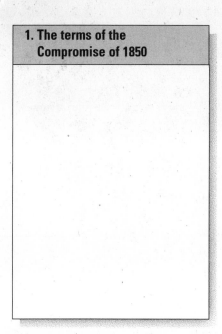

1. The terms of the Compromise of 1850	2. The role played by the following figures in the Compromise
	Henry Clay
	John C. Calhoun
	Daniel Webster
	Stephen Douglas

B. On the back of this paper, explain what the **Wilmot Proviso** was, identify who **Millard Fillmore** was, and discuss the relationship that existed between **secession** and the concept of **popular sovereignty.**

Name _____ Date _____

A. As you read, make notes to answer questions about the issue of slavery.

After the Compromise of 1850 is reached, Northern abolitionists continue to attack slavery.

In reaction to the Fugitive Slave Act, Northern states pass personal liberty laws.	Harriet Tubman conducts more than 300 slaves to freedom on the Underground Railroad.	Harriet Beecher Stowe describes slavery's evils in her novel, *Uncle Tom's Cabin.*

The North-South split grows deeper.
Stephen Douglas proposes replacing the Missouri Compromise with the Kansas-Nebraska Act.

1. How had the Missouri Compromise proposed to limit slavery?	2. How did the Kansas-Nebraska Act propose to deal with the issue of slavery?

The Kansas-Nebraska Act is passed in 1852.

3. Why did Douglas believe that popular sovereignty would solve the problem of slavery in the Nebraska Territory?	4. Why did popular sovereignty, in fact, lead to "Bleeding Kansas," instead of settling the issue of slavery in the Nebraska Territory?

B. On the back of this paper, explain why **John Brown** is an important figure in U.S. history.

Name _____ Date _____

CHAPTER
10
Section 3

GUIDED READING *The Birth of the*
Republican Party

A. As you read about political changes in the mid-19th century, fill out the chart below by writing answers in the appropriate boxes.

1834	The Whig Party is formed and then splits over the slavery issue.	
1848	The Free-Soil Party is formed. →	**1.** What did the Free-Soilers oppose? Why?
1854	The Know-Nothing Party, formed to promote nativism, is soon split over the slavery issue. →	**2.** What did the Know-Nothings oppose? Why?
	The Republican Party is formed. →	**3.** What did supporters of the Republican Party have in common?
1855	"Bleeding Kansas"	**4.** What made the party strong?
1856	In the presidential election, Democrat James Buchanan defeats Republican John C. Frémont and the Know-Nothing candidate, Millard Filmore. →	**5.** What did the election indicate about the Democrats?
	→	**6.** What did the election indicate about the Republicans?

B. On the back of this paper, briefly identify **Horace Greeley** and **Franklin Pierce.**

Name _____ Date _____

A. As you read about reasons for the South's secession, fill out the chart below.

	Supporters	**Reasons for their Support**
1. Dred Scott decision	❑ Proslavery forces ❑ Antislavery forces	
2. Lecompton constitution	❑ Proslavery forces ❑ Antislavery forces	
3. Douglas, in the Lincoln-Douglas debates	❑ Proslavery forces ❑ Antislavery forces	
4. Lincoln, in the Lincoln-Douglas debates	❑ Proslavery forces ❑ Antislavery forces	
5. The raid on Harpers Ferry	❑ Proslavery forces ❑ Antislavery forces	
6. John Brown's hanging	❑ Proslavery forces ❑ Antislavery forces	
7. The election of Lincoln to the presidency	❑ Proslavery forces ❑ Antislavery forces	
8. The secession of Southern states	❑ Proslavery forces ❑ Antislavery forces	

B. On the back of this paper, note something important that you learned about the following:

Roger B. Taney   **Freeport Doctrine**   **Confederacy**   **Jefferson Davis**

Name _____   Date _____

CHAPTER
11
Section 1

GUIDED READING *The Civil War Begins*

A. As you read about the outbreak of the Civil War, summarize the advantages held
by each side at the time war was declared.

1. What advantages did the Union have?	2. What advantages did the Confederacy have?

B. Fill in the chart below with information about four early battles of the Civil War.
(Two answers have already been provided.)

	Head of Union Forces	Head of Confederate Forces	Outcome of the Battle	Important Facts
1. Fort Sumter		Beauregard		
2. Bull Run				
3. Shiloh		Johnson and Beauregard		
4. Antietam				

C. On the back of this paper, briefly explain what the **Anaconda plan** was and who
David G. Farragut was.

Name _____ Date _____

A. As you read about wartime politics, briefly note the causes or effects (depending
on which is missing) of each situation.

Causes	Effects
1. Great Britain had little need for Southern cotton, since it possessed a large cotton inventory and had found new sources of raw cotton. The failure of the English wheat crop made Northern wheat an essential import. British popular opinion opposed slavery, especially after the Emancipation Proclamation.	
2.	Lincoln issues the Emancipation Proclamation.
3.	Lincoln suspends the writ of *habeas corpus* in the state of Maryland.
4.	Both the Union and Confederate governments pass draft laws.
5. A draft law was passed favoring and protecting the wealthy. Lower-class white workers were angered about having to fight a war to free slaves who, they believed, would then take over their jobs. Low wages, bad living conditions, and high unemployment among the lower class stirred up a mob mentality and racism.	

B. On the back of this paper, briefly define the following:

Copperhead   **conscription**

CHAPTER 11
Section 3

GUIDED READING *Life During Wartime*

A. As you read, make notes in the boxes to describe the changes caused by the war.

How wartime affected . . .	
1. Southern slaves	2. Southern economy
3. Northern economy	4. Soldiers on both sides
5. African-American soldiers in the North	6. White women in the North and in the South
7. Taxation in the North	8. Health care

B. On the back of this paper, write what you think is important about the following:

Fort Pillow   **Andersonville**   **Clara Barton**

GUIDED READING *The North Takes Charge*

As you read about why the Union won the war, make notes to answer the questions.

1863	Chancellorsville	→	1. What did the Confederacy win at Chancellorsville? What did it lose?
	Gettysburg	→	2. Why is Gettysburg considered a turning point in the war?
	Vicksburg and Port Hudson	→	3. What did the Union accomplish by capturing Vicksburg and Port Hudson?
	Gettysburg Address	→	4. What did the Gettysburg Address help Americans to realize?
1864	Grant is appointed commander of all Union armies.	→	5. What was Grant's overall strategy for defeating Lee's army? What tactics did he use?
	Sherman's march from Atlanta to the sea	→	6. What was Sherman's goal in his march to the sea? What tactics did he use to accomplish that goal?
	Lincoln is reelected.		
	Appomattox	→	7. What were the North's terms of surrender? Why were they so generous to the South?

Name _____ Date _____

CHAPTER
11
Section 5

GUIDED READING *The Legacy of the War*

A. As you read about the consequences of the Civil War, make notes to trace the effects of the war on different aspects of American life.

Effects of the Civil War . . .
1. On political life
2. On the nation's economy
3. On soldiers and civilians
4. On African Americans

B. On the back of this paper, briefly identify each of the following:

Thirteenth Amendment   **John Wilkes Booth**

Name _____ Date _____

A. As you read about Reconstruction policies, make notes to answer the questions.

1865	Lincoln is assassinated. Johnson announces his Reconstruction plan. Congress convenes, excluding newly elected Southerners.	→	1. What did Johnson's Reconstruction plan call for?

| **1866** | Congress votes to continue and to enlarge the Freedmen's Bureau. | → | 2. What was the purpose of the Freedmen's Bureau? |

| | Congress passes the Civil Rights Act of 1866.
Johnson vetoes the Freedmen's Bureau Bill and the Civil Rights Act. | → | 3. What were the provisions of the Civil Rights Act? |

| | Congress overrides the vetoes and adopts the Fourteenth Amendment. | → | 4. What were the main provisions of the Fourteenth Amendment? |

| | Congressional elections are held. | → | 5. What was the central issue of the 1866 congressional elections? |

| **1867** | Congress passes the Reconstruction Act.
Johnson vetoes the Reconstruction Act. | → | 6. What were the main features of the act? |

| | Congress overrides the veto.
Johnson is impeached. | → | 7. Why was Johnson impeached? What was the Senate's verdict after his impeachment trial? |

| **1868** | Grant is elected President.
Congress adopts the Fifteenth Amendment. | → | 8. What did the Fifteenth Amendment guarantee? |

B. On the back of this paper, identify the following:

Radical Republicans   **Thaddeus Stevens**   **Wade–Davis Bill**

Name _____ Date _____

CHAPTER 12
Section 2

GUIDED READING *Reconstructing Society*

A. As you read this section, make notes that summarize postwar changes in the South. List the problems that the region suffered, grouping each problem according to whether it was mainly political, economic, or social. Then indicate how individuals and the government responded to each difficulty or crisis.

Problems	Responses
1. Primarily political	
2. Primarily economic	
3. Primarily social	

B. On the back of this paper, identify or explain each of the following:

Hiram Revels   scalawag   carpetbagger   sharecropping   tenant farming

Reconstruction and Its Effects 51

Name _____ Date _____

A. As you read about the end of Reconstruction, make notes in the chart to explain
how each trend or event contributed to its collapse.

1. The rise of the Ku Klux Klan and other white supremacy groups	
2. The use of intimidation against Republican voters in Mississippi, Florida, South Carolina, and Louisiana	
3. Congress's approval of both the Amnesty Act and the end of the Freedmen's Bureau	
4. The exposure of widespread corruption in the Grant administration	
5. The formation of the Liberal Republican Party and the presidential campaign of 1872	
6. The Panic of 1873, economic depression, and currency controversies	
7. The Supreme Court decisions handed down in the *Slaughterhouse* cases, *U.S.* v. *Cruikshank*, and *U.S.* v. *Reese*	
8. The deaths of such Radical Republican leaders as Charles Sumner and Thaddeus Stevens	
9. The Compromise of 1877 (the political deal reached between supporters of Hayes and Tilden)	

B. On the back of this paper, briefly define **redemption** and **home rule**.

Name _____ Date _____

GUIDED READING *Cultures Clash on the Prairie*

CHAPTER **13**
Section 1

A. As you read about the conflicts that occurred during the settlement of the Western frontier, answer questions about the time line below.

1858	Discovery of Gold in Colorado →	1. How did the discovery of gold affect the settlement of the West?
1864	Sand Creek Massacre →	2. What happened at Sand Creek?
1868	Treaty of Fort Laramie →	3. What were the terms of the Treaty of Fort Laramie? Why did it fail?
1874	Invasion by gold miners of the Sioux's sacred Black Hills	
1876	George A. Custer's Last Stand →	4. What happened at the Battle of Little Bighorn?
1887	The policy of assimilation formalized in the Dawes Act →	5. What was the purpose of the Dawes Act?
1890	The Spread of the Ghost Dance movement; the death of Sitting Bull; the Battle of Wounded Knee →	6. What happened at Wounded Knee Creek?

B. On the back of this paper, identify **Sitting Bull** and describe how he tried to deal with the problems his people faced.

Name _____ Date _____

GUIDED READING *Settling on the Great Plains*

A. As you read this section, note how each of the factors listed below (Causes) helped to settle the West and turned the eastern Great Plains into the nation's "breadbasket" (Effects).

Causes	Effects
1. Land grants given to the railroads	
2. The Homestead Act and related laws passed in the 1870s	
3. Inventions and improvements in farm technology	
4. The Morrill Land Grant Acts and Hatch Act	

B. What were some hardships faced by frontier farmers? (Note: one hardship per box)

C. On the back of this paper, explain **homesteader, soddy,** and **bonanza farm.**

Name _____ Date _____

GUIDED READING *Farmers and the Populist Movement*

Section 3

A. As you read this section, take notes to answer questions about the pressures that made farming increasingly unprofitable.

In the late 1800s, farmers faced increasing costs and decreasing crop prices.

1. Why had farming become unprofitable during this period?	2. Why did farmers support bimetallism or "free silver"?

In 1892, farmers and farm organizations, such as the Grange, found support in Populism and the People's Party.

3. What economic reforms did the People's Party call for?	4. What political reforms did the party call for?

In 1896, the Populists supported presidential candidate William Jennings Bryan.

5. What factions did Bryan and the Populists see as opposing forces in the presidential election of 1896?	6. In what ways did the results of the 1896 election confirm this view?

B. On the back of this paper, note who **Mary Elizabeth Lease** and **Oliver Hudson Kelley** were. Then, briefly explain the relationship between **inflation/deflation** and the **"Cross of Gold"** speech.

CHAPTER 14

Section 1

GUIDED READING *The Expansion of Industry*

After the Civil War, the United States was still a mostly rural nation. By the 1920s, it had become the leading industrial nation of the world. This immense change was caused by three major factors. Answer the questions for two of the factors.

➤ **Factor 1: Abundant Natural Resources**

1. Which resources played crucial roles in industrialization?	2. How did Edwin L. Drake help industry to acquire larger quantities of oil?	3. How did the Bessemer process allow better use of iron ore?	4. What new uses for steel were developed at this time?

➤ **Factor 2: Increasing Number of Inventions**

5. How did Thomas Alva Edison contribute to this development?	6. How did George Westinghouse contribute to it?	7. How did Christopher Sholes contribute?	8. How did Alexander Graham Bell contribute?

➤ **Factor 3: Expanding Urban Population**

Provided markets for new inventions and industrial goods	Provided a ready supply of labor for industry

Name _____ Date _____

A. As you read, take notes to answer questions about the growth of the railroads.

Realizing that railroads were critical to the settlement of the West and the development of the nation, the federal government made huge land grants and loans to the railroad companies.

| **Benefits** → | The railroad companies built transcontinental and local lines. | The nation was transformed from a collection of regions into a united nation. | Railroad time became the nation's standard, linking Americans in one more way. |

| **Drawbacks** → | The unchecked power and greed of the railroad companies led to widespread corruption and abuse of power. |

1. What problems did employees of the railroad companies face?	2. What was it like to live as a Pullman employee in the town of Pullman?
3. Who was involved in Crédit Mobilier, and what was the purpose of this company?	4. In what ways did the railroad companies use their power to hurt farmers?
5. Why didn't the decision in the *Munn* v. *Illinois* case succeed in checking the power of the railroads?	6. Why didn't the Interstate Commerce Act immediately limit the power of the railroads?

B. On the back of this paper, explain the importance to the United States of the **transcontinental railroad.** Then, describe who **George M. Pullman** was and why he is a significant historical figure.

Name _____ Date _____

CHAPTER 14

Section 3

GUIDED READING *Big Business and Labor*

As you read this section, answer the questions below about government's attempts to regulate big business.

a. What is it?

b. How did it help businesses such as the Carnegie Company and tycoons like Andrew Carnegie?

1. Vertical integration	a. b.
2. Horizontal integration	a. b.
3. Social Darwinism	a. b.
4. Monopoly	a. b.
5. Holding company	a. b.
6. Trust	a. b.

c. How did it harm businesses such as Standard Oil and tycoons like John D. Rockefeller?

7. The perception of tycoons as "robber barons"	
8. Sherman Antitrust Act	

Name _____ Date _____

A. As you read about people who immigrated to the United States in the late 19th
and early 20th centuries, write notes to answer the questions below.

Immigrants from . . .	What were some of the countries they came from?	What reasons did they often have for coming to the U.S.?	Where did they often enter the U.S.?
1. Southern and Eastern Europe			❒ Ellis Island ❒ Angel Island ❒ Southeastern U.S. ❒ Southwestern U.S.
2. Asia			❒ Ellis Island ❒ Angel Island ❒ Southeastern U.S. ❒ Southwestern U.S.
3. Caribbean Islands and Central America			❒ Ellis Island ❒ Angel Island ❒ Southeastern U.S. ❒ Southwestern U.S.

B. In each box below, identify an important difference that tended to exist between native-
born Americans and some or all of the new immigrants around the turn of the century.

Native-Born	New Immigrants

C. On the back of this paper, explain the purposes of the **Chinese Exclusion Act** and
the **Gentlemen's Agreement.**

Name _____ Date _____

GUIDED READING *The Challenges of Urbanization*

A. As you read about the rapid growth of American cities in the late 19th and early
20th centuries, take notes to answer the questions below.

The People	Why was each group drawn to cities in the Northeast and Midwest?
1. Immigrants	
2. Farmers	
3. African Americans	

The Problems	What was done in response to each problem?
4. Lack of safe and efficient transportation	
5. Unsafe drinking water	
6. Lack of sanitation	
7. Fire hazards	
8. Crime	

B. On the back of this paper, define **urbanization.** Then, explain how the **Social
Gospel movement, settlement houses,** and **Jane Addams** were involved in
efforts to solve the problems of urbanization.

Name _____ Date _____

CHAPTER 15

Section 3

GUIDED READING *Politics in the Gilded Age*

A. As you read this section, fill out the chart below by writing answers to questions about the Gilded Age.

1876	**Rutherford B. Hayes elected president** →	1. What was Hayes's position on civil service reform? What did he do to promote it?
1880	**James A. Garfield elected president** →	2. In the debate over civil service reform, did Garfield seem to favor the Stalwarts or the reformers?
1881	**Garfield assassinated; Chester A. Arthur assumes the presidency** →	3. What position did Arthur take on civil service reform, and what did he do to support it?
1883	**Pendleton Act passed** →	4. What did the Pendleton Act do?
1884	**Grover Cleveland elected president** →	5. What was Cleveland's position on tariffs, and what did he do to promote this position?
1888	**Benjamin Harrison elected president** →	6. What was Harrison's position on tariffs, and what did he do to support that stand?
1892	**Cleveland reelected president** →	7. What happened to tariffs during Cleveland's second presidency?
1897	**William McKinley elected president** →	8. What happened to tariffs during McKinley's presidency?

B. On the back of this paper, define **political machine** and describe how it worked.

Immigrants and Urbanization 61

Name _____ Date _____

GUIDED READING *Science and Urban Life*

Section 1

A. As you read about how technological changes at the turn of the 20th century affected American life, write notes in the appropriate boxes. Leave the shaded boxes blank.

	1. Who was involved in its development?	2. What other inventions helped make this one possible?	3. How did this invention or development affect Americans' lives?
Skyscraper			
Electric transit			
Suspension bridge			
Urban planning			
Airmail			
Web-perfecting press			
Kodak camera			

B. On the back of this paper, explain how **Central Park** can be considered an achievement in science.

Name _____ Date _____

GUIDED READING *Expanding Public Education*

A. As you read this section, write notes to describe the chief characteristics of each type of educational institution and the developments that took place at the turn of the 20th century.

	Chief Characteristics and Important Developments
1. Elementary schools	
2. High schools	
3. Colleges and universities	
4. Education for immigrant adults	

B. On the back of this paper, briefly describe the contribution of each of the following people to American education during this time.

W. E. B. Du Bois   **Booker T. Washington**   **Henry Ford**

Name _____ Date _____

GUIDED READING *Segregation and Discrimination*

Section 3

A. As you read about racial tensions at the turn of the 20th century, write notes to answer the questions.

	In what region or regions did it exist?	Who were its targets?	How did it affect the lives of these people?
1. Literacy test			
2. Poll tax			
3. Grandfather clause			
4. Jim Crow laws			
5. Racial etiquette			
6. Debt peonage			
7. Chinese Exclusion Act			

B. On the back of this paper, explain why **Ida B. Wells** is a significant historical figure and note what the Supreme Court said about **segregation** in *Plessy v. Ferguson.*

Name _____ Date _____

CHAPTER 16

Section 4

GUIDED READING *The Dawn of Mass Culture*

A. As you read about the emergence of modern mass culture, give *either* an example of each item *or* mention one of the people who invented or popularized it. Then note one reason why the item became so popular around the turn of the 20th century.

	1. Amusement parks	2. Bicycling	3. Boxing	4. Baseball
Example				
Reason				

	5. Shopping centers	6. Department stores	7. Chain stores	8. Mail-order catalogs
Example				
Reason				

B. On the back of this paper, describe the impact that **rural free delivery** had on the country.

CHAPTER
17
Section 1

GUIDED READING *The Origins of Progressivism*

A. As you read about the era of reform, take notes about the goals, reformers, and successes of the reform movements.

Social Reforms	People and Groups Involved	Successes (laws, legal decisions, etc.)
1. Social welfare reform movement		
2. Moral reform movement		
3. Economic reform movement		
4. Movement for industrial efficiency		
5. Movement to protect workers		

Political Reforms	People and Groups Involved	Successes (laws, legal decisions, etc.)
6. Movement to reform local government		
7. State reform of big business		
8. Movement for election reform		

B. On the back of this paper, explain the importance of the following:

progressive movement   **prohibition**   **scientific management**

Name _____   Date _____

CHAPTER 17
Section 2

GUIDED READING *Women in Public Life*

A. As you read this section, take notes to answer the questions.

1. What types of jobs were women in each group likely to hold?			
Lower Class	Middle and Upper Class	African American	Immigrant

2. How did educational opportunities for middle- and upper-class women change?

3. How did these new opportunities affect the lives of middle- and upper-class women?

4. What three strategies were adopted by the suffragists to win the vote?		
a.	b.	c.

5. What results did each strategy produce?		
a.	b.	c.

B. On the back of this paper, explain the significance of each of the following:

   NACW   **Susan B. Anthony**   **NAWSA**

Name _____ Date _____

A. As you read this section, write notes to answer questions about President
Theodore Roosevelt. If Roosevelt took no steps to solve the problem or if no
legislation was involved in solving the problem, write "none."

Problem	What steps did Roosevelt take to solve each problem?	Which legislation helped solve the problem?
1. 1902 coal strike		
2. Trusts		
3. Unregulated big business		
4. Dangerous foods and medicines		
5. Shrinking wilderness and natural resources		
6. Racial discrimination		

B. On the back of this paper, explain the importance of each of the following:

Square Deal   *The Jungle*   **Upton Sinclair**   **NAACP**

Name _____ Date _____

CHAPTER 17
Section 4

GUIDED READING *Progressivism Under Taft*

A. As you read this section, take notes to answer questions about growing conflicts between reform and business interests.

In 1912, the Republican Party splits at its convention.

	Progressives	**Conservatives**
1. Why did they support or oppose Taft?		
2. What party did they form or stay with?		

In the 1912 election, four parties run candidates.

	Progressive Party	**Republican Party**	**Democratic Party**	**Socialist Party**
3. Who did they run for president?				
4. What was their candidate's position on big business?				

B. On the back of this paper, explain why **Gifford Pinchot** is an important figure in U.S. history.

Name _____ Date _____

GUIDED READING *Wilson's New Freedom*

As you read about President Wilson's approach to reform, take notes
to answer the questions.

What were the aims of each piece of legislation or constitutional amendment?	
1. Federal Trade Act	
2. Clayton Antitrust Act	
3. Underwood Tariff	
4. Sixteenth Amendment	
5. Federal Reserve Act	

6. Which three new developments finally brought the success of the woman suffrage movement within reach?
7. Which constitutional amendment recognized women's right to vote?

8. How did Wilson retreat on civil rights?

Name _____   Date _____

CHAPTER 18 Section 1

GUIDED READING *Imperialism and America*

A. As you read this section, fill out the chart below by summarizing reasons why the United States became an imperial power.

The Roots of American Imperialism		
1. Economic roots	2. Political and military roots	3. Racist roots

↓

4. What did Admiral Mahan urge the United States to do to protect its interests?

B. For each year on the time line below, identify one important event in the history of U.S. involvement in Hawaii.

U.S. Imperialism in Hawaii	
1875	
1887	
1890	
1891	
1897	
1898	

C. On the back of this paper, identify who **Queen Liliuokalani** and **Sanford B. Dole** were and explain how their lives were connected.

CHAPTER
18
Section 2

GUIDED READING *The Spanish-American War*

A. As you read about the Spanish-American War, write notes in the appropriate boxes to answer the questions about its causes and effects.

Causes: How did each of the following help to cause the outbreak of the Spanish-American War?
1. American business owners
2. José Martí
3. Valeriano Weyler
4. Yellow journalism
5. De Lôme letter
6. U.S.S. *Maine*

Effects: What happened to each of the following territories as a result of the Spanish-American War?
7. Cuba
8. Puerto Rico
9. Guam
10. Philippine Islands

B. On the back of this paper, explain briefly who **George Dewey** was and what he did. Then explain the importance of the **Rough Riders** and **San Juan Hill.**

Name _____ Date _____

A. As you read about America's relations with lands under its influence, write notes to
answer the questions below. Some answers have already been filled in for you.

	Puerto Rico 1898–1916	Cuba 1898–1903	The Philippines 1898–1945	China 1900
1. What was its relationship to the U.S.?	very similar to that of a colony or protectorate			
2. Why did the U.S. try to control its affairs?			to provide the U.S. with raw materials and new markets	
3. What laws and policies affected its relationship with the U.S.?				
4. What violent events affected its relationship with the U.S.?	Spanish- American War			

B. John Hay's "Open Door notes" paved the way for greater U.S. influence in Asia.
Note three beliefs held by Americans that were reflected by the Open Door policy.

1.
2.
3.

C. On the back of this paper, briefly note who **Emilio Aguinaldo** was and how he
affected U.S. foreign policy at the turn of the century.

CHAPTER 18 **Section 4**

GUIDED READING *America as a World Power*

A. As you read this section, write notes summarizing the effects of American military, diplomatic, and economic power around the world.

ROOSEVELT'S "BIG STICK" DIPLOMACY

American action taken	Consequences of that action
1. Treaty of Portsmouth is negotiated.	
2. U.S. warships are used to ensure Panama's independence.	
3. Panama Canal is built.	
4. Roosevelt Corollary is adopted.	

WILSON'S "MISSIONARY" DIPLOMACY

American action taken	Consequences of that action
5. Wilson uses a minor incident with Mexico as an excuse to occupy Veracruz.	
6. Wilson recognizes the Carranza government.	
7. Wilson refuses Carranza's demand to withdraw U.S. troops sent into Mexico to capture Villa.	

B. On the back of this paper, identify **Francisco "Pancho" Villa** and **John J. Pershing**, and describe how their lives came to be interrelated.

Name _____ Date _____

CHAPTER 19
Section 1

GUIDED READING *World War I Begins*

A. As you read this section, take notes to answer questions about the international politics that led to war in Europe.

How did the following help to ignite the war in Europe?				
1. Nationalism	2. Imperialism	3. Militarism	4. Alliances	5. Assassination of Archduke Ferdinand

Why did the following groups of Americans tend to oppose U.S. participation in the war?			
6. Naturalized citizens	7. Socialists	8. Pacifists	9. Parents

What did the following nations do to encourage U.S. participation in the war?		
10. Britain	11. Germany	12. Russia

B. On the back of this paper, identify or define each of the following:

Allies   **Central Powers**   **"no man's land"**   **trench warfare**   **Zimmermann note**

Name _____ Date _____

GUIDED READING *American Power*
Tips the Balance

CHAPTER
19
Section 2

A. As you read this section, write notes to answer questions about the American experience in World War I.

1. How did the United States raise an army?	2. How did U.S. soldiers help win the war?
3. How did the United States build its naval force?	4. How did the U.S. Navy help win the war?

5. What new weapons of mechanized warfare threatened those in combat?

6. What did the war cost in terms of the number of . . .				7. What were the estimated economic costs?
civilian deaths?	military deaths?	injuries?	refugees?	

B. On the back of this paper, identify or define each of the following:

Alvin York   **conscientious objector**   **Eddie Rickenbacker**

Name _____ Date _____

GUIDED READING *The War at Home*

A. As you read this section, take notes to answer questions about how World War I changed American society.

What were some things accomplished by the following wartime agencies and laws?		
1. War Industries Board	2. Railroad Administration	3. Fuel Administration
4. National War Labor Board	5. Food Administration	6. Committee on Public Information
7. Espionage and Sedition Acts		

What changes did the war bring about for the following groups of Americans?		
8. Immigrants	9. African Americans	10. Women

B. On the back of this paper, briefly explain why **Bernard M. Baruch** and **George Creel** are significant historical figures.

Name _____ Date _____

CHAPTER 19

Section 4

GUIDED READING *Wilson Fights for Peace*

As you read about President Wilson's plan for world peace, make notes to answer questions related to the time line below.

1918	Wilson delivers Fourteen Points speech to Congress. →	What were Wilson's points? 1. 2. 3. 4. 5. 6.–13. 14.
1919	Treaty of Versailles is signed. →	15. What terms of the treaty specifically affected Germany? 16. What were the weaknesses of the treaty?
1920	Senate rejects Treaty of Versailles. →	17. Why did Henry Cabot Lodge object to the treaty?
1921	Senate again rejects Treaty of Versailles. →	18. How did Wilson help bring about the Senate's rejection of the treaty?
	U.S. signs separate treaty with Germany. →	19. What circumstances at this time would eventually lead many Germans to support Adolf Hitler?

Name _____ Date _____

CHAPTER 20
Section 1

GUIDED READING *Americans Struggle with Postwar Issues*

A. As you read this section, take notes to answer questions about postwar conditions in America and the fear of communism.

After World War I, many Americans feared that Communists would take over the country.

1. How did the Justice Department under A. Mitchell Palmer respond to this fear?	2. Why did Palmer eventually lose his standing with the American public?
3. How did the Ku Klux Klan respond to this fear?	4. Why did the Klan eventually lose popularity and membership?

Public opinion turned against labor unions as many Americans came to believe that unions encouraged communism.

5. Why was the strike by Boston police unpopular with the public?	6. Why did Massachusetts governor Calvin Coolidge become so popular?
7. Why was the strike at U.S. Steel unpopular?	8. How did President Wilson respond to the steel strike?

The American labor union movement suffered setbacks as union membership dropped.

B. On the back of this paper, briefly describe how **Sacco and Vanzetti** became victims of the Red Scare. Then explain how **John L. Lewis** improved the lives of coal miners.

Name _____ Date _____

GUIDED READING *The Harding Presidency*

A. On the back of this page, note four measures taken by the Harding administration to maintain world peace.

B. Complete this description of how the Fordney-McCumber Tariff worked against Harding's efforts to maintain world peace. On each blank, write **B** for Britain, **F** for France, **G** for Germany, or **U** for the United States.

(1)___ adopted the Fordney-McCumber Tariff to protect businesses in (2)___ from foreign competition. This tariff made it difficult for (3)___ and (4)___ to sell goods in (5)___ and, therefore, difficult to repay their war debts to (6)___. To get money to pay those debts, they demanded reparations from (7)___, and troops from (8)___ invaded the Ruhr, an industrial region of (9)___. To avoid a new war, (10)___ adopted the Dawes Plan. Under this program, investors from (11)___ made loans to (12)___. It used the money to repay war debts to (13)___ and (14)___. Then they used the same money to repay war debts to banks in (15)___. In effect, (16)___ was repaid with its own money. This arrangement caused bad feelings on both sides of the Atlantic.

C. In the blank boxes below, write one or two words that describe how each nation, person, or group felt about the issues listed.

1. Americans → Kellogg-Briand Pact		2. Britain and France → Dawes Plan	
3. Americans → Immigrants		4. Ohio gang → Public service	
5. Harding → Administration scandals		6. Americans → Harding	

D. On the back of this page, note how the actions of **Charles Evans Hughes** and **Albert B. Fall** affected the reputation of the Harding administration.

Name _____ Date _____

CHAPTER 20

Section 3

GUIDED READING *The Business of America*

A. In the first column, write notes to describe how the inventions and trends of the 1920s changed American life. In the second column, write the name of a related company or product that contributed to the boom of the 1920s.

Invention or Trend	Effects of the Invention or Trend	Company or Product
1. Automobiles		
2. Airplane industry		
3. Alternating electrical current		
4. Modern advertising		
5. Installment plan		

B. Why should Americans in the 1920s have shown greater concern for their future? Note three things that were, or might have been, seen as "clouds in the blue skies of prosperity."

1.	2.	3.

C. On the back of this paper, explain the meaning of **urban sprawl.**

Name _____ Date _____

GUIDED READING *Changing Ways of Life*

As you read about how the 1920s reflected conflicts and tensions in American culture, take notes to answer the questions below.

In January 1920, prohibition went into effect.

1. a. Who tended to be supporters of prohibition at this time? b. Why did they support it?	2. a. Who tended to be opponents of prohibition at this time? b. Why did they oppose it?
3. Why was prohibition repealed?	

In July 1925, Clarence Darrow and William Jennings Bryan faced each other in the Scopes trial.

4. a. Who were Darrow's main supporters? b. Why did they support him?	5. a. Who were Bryan's main supporters? b. Why did they support him?
6. What was the outcome of the case?	

Name _____ Date _____

A. As you read about women's changing roles in the 1920s, fill out the chart by writing notes in the appropriate spaces.

Social Life in the 1920s	
1. Note two ways women's fashions changed.	
2. Note two ways women's social behavior changed.	
3. Note two words that describe the attitude reflected by these changes.	

Work and Home Life in the 1920s	
4. Note one way women's work opportunities improved.	
5. Note two ways women's home and family life improved.	

6. Note three negative effects that accompanied women's changing roles in the 1920s.	

B. On the back of this paper, define **flapper** and **double standard**.

Name _____ Date _____

GUIDED READING *Education and Popular Culture*

Section 3

A. As you read this section, take notes summarizing how public education changed.

	Education Before the 1920s	Education During the 1920s
1. Enrollments		
2. Types of courses		
3. Immigrants		
4. Financing		

B. As you read about how America's popular culture developed in the 1920s, give at least two specific examples of each area of popular culture.

1. Magazines	2. Radio
3. Sports	4. Movies
5. Theater, music, and art	6. Literature

C. On the back of this paper, briefly explain who **Charles A. Lindbergh** was and how he became America's "most beloved hero" of the 1920s.

CHAPTER 21

Section 4

GUIDED READING *The Harlem Renaissance*

A. Name the organization with which each leader was associated. Then note their beliefs and goals as well as the tactics they believed necessary to achieve them.

1. **W. E. B. Du Bois and James Weldon Johnson**	2. **Marcus Garvey**
Organization:	Organization:
Beliefs, goals, and tactics:	Beliefs, goals, and tactics:

B. Describe briefly what each of the following artists was known for.

African-American Writers
1. Claude McKay
2. Langston Hughes
3. Zora Neale Hurston

African-American Performers
4. Paul Robeson
5. Louis Armstrong
6. Duke Ellington
7. Bessie Smith

Name _____ Date _____

CHAPTER 22

Section 1

GUIDED READING *The Nation's Sick Economy*

A. As you read this section, take notes to describe the serious problems in each area of the economy that helped cause the Great Depression.

1. Industry	2. Agriculture

3. Consumer spending	4. Distribution of wealth	5. Stock market

B. On the back of this paper, explain or define each of the following:

Alfred E. Smith   Dow Jones Industrial Average

Black Tuesday   Hawley-Smoot Tariff Act

Name _____ Date _____

CHAPTER
22
Section 2

GUIDED READING *Hardship and Suffering During the Depression*

A. As you read about how people coped with hard times, use the chart below to summarize the Great Depression's effects on various aspects of American life.

1. Employment
2. Housing
3. Farming
4. Race relations
5. Family life
6. Physical health
7. Emotional health

B. On the back of this paper, define each of the following terms.

Dust Bowl   **shantytown**   **soup kitchen**   **bread line**   **direct relief**

Name _____ Date _____

CHAPTER 22
Section 3

GUIDED READING *Hoover Struggles with the Depression*

A. As you read about President Hoover's response to the Great Depression, write notes in the appropriate boxes to answer the questions.

Philosophy
1. What was Hoover's philosophy of government?

Responses and Economic Results
2. What was Hoover's initial reaction to the stock market crash of 1929?
3. a. What was the nation's economic situation in 1930? b. How did voters in 1930 respond to this situation?
4. a. What did Hoover do about the economic situation? b. How did the economy respond to his efforts?
5. a. How did Hoover deal with the economic problem posed by the Bonus Army? b. How did his efforts affect his own political situation?

B. On the back of this paper, explain the the main purpose of the **Reconstruction Finance Corporation** (RFC) and whether it succeeded in achieving that goal.

Name _____ Date _____

A. As you read about President Roosevelt's New Deal, take notes to answer questions about each new federal program. The first one is done for you.

Federal Program	What was its immediate purpose?	What was its long-term goal?
Business Assistance and Reform		
1. Emergency Banking Relief Act (EBRA)	Authorized the Treasury Department to inspect and close banks	To restore public confidence in banks
2. Glass-Steagall Banking Act of 1933		
3. Federal Securities Act		
4. National Industrial Recovery Act (NIRA)		
Farm Relief/Rural Development		
5. Agricultural Adjustment Act (AAA)		
6. Tennessee Valley Authority (TVA)		
Employment Projects		
7. Civilian Conservation Corps (CCC)		
8. Federal Emergency Relief Administration (FERA)		
9. Public Works Administration (PWA)		
10. Civil Works Administration (CWA)		
Housing		
11. Home Owners Loan Corporation (HOLC)		

B. On the back of this paper, explain who **Huey Long** was and why he is a significant historical figure.

Name _____ Date _____

GUIDED READING *The Second New Deal*
Takes Hold

A. As you read this section, take notes to answer questions about the second phase of
Roosevelt's New Deal policies.

Group	What problems did each group face during the Depression?	What laws were passed and agencies established to deal with these problems?
1. Farmers, migrant workers, and others living in rural areas		
2. Students and other young people		
3. Teachers, writers, artists, and other professionals		
4. All workers, including the unemployed		
5. Retired workers		
6. The disabled, the needy elderly, and dependent mothers and children		

B. On the back of this paper, describe how **Eleanor Roosevelt** contributed to the
nation's recovery from the Depression.

Name _____ Date _____

GUIDED READING *The New Deal Affects Many Groups*

A. As you read, write notes about each group in Roosevelt's New Deal coalition.

1. Women Example(s) of appointees to important government positions:	Gains women made under the New Deal:	Problems of women not solved by the New Deal:

2. African Americans Example(s) of appointees to important government positions:	Gains African Americans made under the New Deal:	Problems of African Americans not solved by the New Deal:

3. Labor unions Example(s) of union(s) organized during the New Deal:	Gains unions made under the New Deal:	Problems of unions not solved by the New Deal:

4. Other coalition groups Other groups:	Reasons they supported the Democratic party:

B. On the back of this paper, explain who **John Collier** was and how he helped one of the New Deal coalition groups.

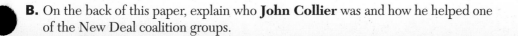

CHAPTER 23

Section 4

GUIDED READING *Culture in the 1930s*

As you read about how the Depression and New Deal influenced American culture, write notes in the appropriate boxes to answer the questions about each work.

Films and Radio Drama		
1. *Gone with the Wind*	What was it? Who created or appeared in it?	What was its theme?
2. *Mr. Smith Goes to Washington*	What was it? Who created or appeared in it?	What was its theme?
3. *The War of the Worlds*	What was it? Who created or appeared in it?	What was its theme?
4. *Waiting for Lefty*	What was it? Who created or appeared in it?	What was its theme?
Art and Literature		
5. *Native Son*	What was it? Who created or appeared in it?	What was its theme?
6. *The Grapes of Wrath*	What was it? Who created or appeared in it?	What was its theme?
7 *Our Town*	What was it? Who created or appeared in it?	What was its theme?
8. *American Gothic*	What was it? Who created or appeared in it?	What was its theme?

CHAPTER 23

Section 5

GUIDED READING *The Impact of the New Deal*

A. As you read about the impact of New Deal reforms, take notes about the lasting effects of those reforms on American society.

	New Deal Laws and Agencies	Lasting Effects of These Laws and Agencies on American Government and Life
1. Labor		
2. Agriculture and rural life		
3. Banking and finance		
4. Social welfare		
5. Environment		

B. On the back of this paper, explain the meaning of **parity.**

Name _____ Date _____

GUIDED READING *Dictators Threaten World Peace*

Section 1

A. As you read this section, take notes about the rise of dictators in Europe and Asia.

	1. Joseph Stalin	2. Benito Mussolini	3. Adolf Hitler
Nation			
Political movement and beliefs			
Aggressive actions taken in the 1920s and 1930s			

	4. Japanese Militarists	5. Francisco Franco
Nation		
Political movement and beliefs		
Aggressive actions taken in the 1920s and 1930s		

B. On the back of this paper, define **totalitarian.** Then explain the significance of the **Neutrality Acts.**

Name _____ Date _____

CHAPTER
24
Section 2

GUIDED READING *War in Europe*

A. As you read this section, take notes to answer questions about how Germany
started World War II. Note the development of events in the time line.

1938		
March	Germany invades Austria.	**1. Why did Neville Chamberlain sign the Munich Pact?** / **2. Why did Winston Churchill oppose the pact?**
September	Munich Pact is signed by Germany, France, and Britain. →	

1939	**3. What did Germany and the USSR agree to in their accords?**
March — Germany invades Czechoslovakia.	
August — Germany and USSR sign nonaggression pact and secret agreement. →	
September — Germany invades Poland. →	**4. What happened to Poland as a result of the invasion, and how did Britain and France respond to it?**
November — USSR invades Finland.	

1940	**5. What were the surrender terms offered to France?**
Spring — Germany invades Norway, Denmark, the Netherlands, Belgium, and Luxembourg.	
June — France surrenders to Germany. →	
Summer — USSR overruns Baltic states.	**6. What type of battle was the Battle of Britain, and why was England's victory so important?**
Battle of Britain begins. →	

B. On the back of this paper, identify who **Charles de Gaulle** was. Then define
appeasement, nonaggression pact, and **blitzkrieg.**

Name _____ Date _____

CHAPTER 24

Section 3

GUIDED READING *The Holocaust*

A. As you read, take notes to answer questions related to the time line.

1925	In *Mein Kampf,* Hitler presents his racist views on "Aryans" and Jews.	
1933	Hitler comes to power. Soon after, he orders non-Aryans to be removed from government jobs and begins to build concentration camps.	
	Thousands of Jews begin leaving Germany. →	1. Why didn't France and Britain accept as many German Jews as they might have?
1935	Nuremberg laws are passed. →	2. What did the Nuremberg laws do?
1938	*Kristallnacht* occurs. →	3. What happened during *Kristallnacht?*
1939	As war breaks out in Europe, U.S. Coast Guard prevents refugees on the *St. Louis* from landing in Miami. →	4. Why didn't the United States accept as many German Jews as it might have?
1941	Nazis build six death camps in Poland. →	5. What groups did the Nazis single out for extermination?
1945 to 1949	After war in Europe ends in 1945, many Nazi leaders are brought to justice for their crimes against humanity. →	6. How did the Nazis go about exterminating the approximately 11 million people who died in the Holocaust?

B. On the back of this paper, define **genocide.**

Name _____ Date _____

CHAPTER
24
Section 4

GUIDED READING *America Moves Toward War*

As you read, take notes about how the United States entered World War II.

1939	Congress passes Neutrality Act.	→	1. What did the Neutrality Act allow?
1940	Axis powers form alliance.	→	2. Who were the Axis powers? What did their alliance mean for the United States?
1941	Congress passes Lend-Lease Act.

Germany invades USSR. | → | 3. What did the Lend-Lease Act do? |
| | Japan takes over French military bases in Indochina.

Congress extends the draft. | → | 4. What did the United States do to protest Japan's action? |
| | Churchill and Roosevelt draft the Atlantic Charter. | → | 5. What pledges were contained in the Atlantic Charter? |
| | "A Declaration by the United Nations" is signed by the Allies.

Hideki Tojo becomes Japan's prime minister. | → | 6. Who were the Allies? |
| | U.S. Senate allows arming of merchant ships.

Japan launches a surprise attack on Pearl Harbor. | → | 7. What did the attack do to the U.S. Pacific fleet? |
| | As U.S. declares war on Japan, Germany and Italy declare war on U.S. | → | 8. Why did Germany and Italy declare war on the United States? |

Name _____ Date _____

CHAPTER 25
Section 1

GUIDED READING *Mobilizing for Defense*

A. As you read about how the United States mobilized for war, note how each of the following contributed to that effort.

1. Selective Service System	6. Office of Scientific Research and Development (OSRD)
2. Women	7. Entertainment industry
3. Minorities	8. Office of Price Administration (OPA)
4. Manufacturers	9. War Production Board (WPB)
5. A. Philip Randolph	10. Rationing

B. On the back of this paper, briefly describe **George Marshall**'s position on how women could contribute to the war effort. Then, explain who the **Nisei** were and what happened to them.

Name _____ Date _____

CHAPTER 25
Section 2

GUIDED READING *The War for Europe and North Africa*

A. As you read about the Allied war effort, take notes to explain what made each event a critical moment or turning point in the war.

February 1943	**End of Battle of Stalingrad** →	1.
May 1943	**End of Operation Torch** →	2.
Mid-1943	**Victory in Battle of the Atlantic** →	3.
June 1944	**D-Day** →	4.
July 1944	**Liberation of Majdanek** →	5.
August 1944	**Liberation of France** →	6.
October 1944	**Capture of Aachen** →	7.
January 1945	**End of Battle of the Bulge** →	8.
Spring 1945	**End of Italian campaign** →	9.
May 1945	**V-E Day** →	10.

B. On the back of this paper, note the official title of each of the following and describe the roles they played during the war.

Dwight D. Eisenhower   **George Patton**   **Harry S. Truman**

Name _____ Date _____

A. As you read about the Allied war effort, take notes to explain what made each
event a critical moment or turning point in the war.

The War in the Pacific		
Date and Place	**Leaders Involved**	**What happened?**
1. April 1942, Bataan		
2. June 1942, Midway		
3. August 1942, Guadalcanal		
4. October 1944, Leyte Gulf		
5. March 1945, Iwo Jima		
6. June 1945, Okinawa		
7. September 1945, Tokyo Bay		

The Science of War		
Date and Place	**Leaders Involved**	**What happened?**
8. July 1945, Los Alamos		
9. August 1945, Hiroshima, Nagasaki		

Planning and Rebuilding for Peace		
Date and Place	**Leaders Involved**	**What happened?**
10. February 1945, Yalta		
11. April 1945, San Francisco		
12. 1945–1949, Nuremberg		

B. On the back of this paper, note the official title of each of the following and
describe the roles they played during the war.

Dwight D. Eisenhower   **George Patton**   **Harry S. Truman**

Name _____ Date _____

CHAPTER 25 Section 4

GUIDED READING *The Home Front*

A. As you read this section, write notes to answer questions about the impact of the war on various segments of American society.

How did the war and its immediate aftermath affect the following?	
1. Labor	2. Agriculture
3. Population centers	4. Family life
5. Returning GIs	

How did these groups react to discrimination and racism during and after the war?
6. African Americans
7. Mexican Americans
8. Japanese Americans

B. On the back of this paper, briefly explain why **James Farmer** is an important historical figure.

CHAPTER 26 **Section 1**

GUIDED READING *Origins of the Cold War*

A. As you read this section, complete the cause-and-effect diagram with the specific U.S. actions made in response to the Soviet actions listed. Use the following terms and names in filling out the diagram:

containment　　**Truman Doctrine**　　**Berlin airlift**　　**NATO**

Cause: Soviet Action

Soviet leader Joseph Stalin refused free elections in Eastern Europe and set up satellite nations.

Effect: U.S. Action

1.

Effect: U.S. Action

2.

Cause: Soviet Action

Soviets blockaded Berlin for almost a year.

Effect: U.S. Action

3.

Effect: U.S. Action

4.

B. On the back of this paper, explain the significance of each of the following terms:

Cold War　　**Marshall Plan**

Name _____ Date _____

CHAPTER 26

Section 2

GUIDED READING *The Cold War Heats Up*

A. As you read this section, fill out the chart below by writing answers to the questions in the appropriate boxes.

	Civil War in China	Civil War in Korea
1. Which side did the United States support, and why?		
2. What did the United States do to affect the outcome of the war?		
3. What was the outcome of the war?		
4. How did the American public react to that outcome, and why?		

B. On the back of this paper, explain the significance of each of the following terms and names:

Mao Zedong   Chiang Kai-shek   Taiwan (Formosa)   38th parallel

CHAPTER
26
Section 3

GUIDED READING *The Cold War at Home*

A. As you read this section, fill out the charts below by writing answers to the questions in the appropriate boxes.

	a. What were they accused of ?	b. How were they affected by the accusations?	c. Do the accusations seem to have been fair? Explain.
1. The Hollywood Ten			
2. Alger Hiss			
3. Ethel and Julius Rosenberg			

McCarthyism		
4. What seems to have motivated it?	5. Why did it succeed at first?	6. Why did it fall out of favor?

B. On the back of this paper, explain the significance of each of the following terms and names:

    HUAC   **blacklist**   **Senator Joseph McCarthy**

Name _____ Date _____

A. As you read this section, write your answers to the question in the appropriate boxes.

	How did the United States react, and why?
1. The Soviet Union exploded its first atomic bomb in 1949.	
2. In 1951, the Iranian prime minister placed the oil industry in Iran under the Iranian government's control.	
3. The Guatemalan head of government gave American-owned land in Guatemala to peasants.	
4. In 1956, Britain, France, and Israel invaded Egypt and occupied the Suez Canal.	
5. Soviet tanks invaded Hungary and fired on protesters in 1956.	
6. In 1957, the Soviet Union launched Sputnik.	
7. In 1960, the Soviet Union brought down an American U-2 piloted by Francis Gary Powers.	

B. On the back of this paper, explain the significance of each of the following terms and names:

H-bomb	brinkmanship	Nikita Khrushchev	Warsaw Pact
CIA	Eisenhower Doctrine	Dwight D. Eisenhower	John Foster Dulles

Name _____ Date _____

GUIDED READING *Postwar America*

A. As you read this section, describe the solutions offered to deal with postwar problems.

1. Problem: Millions of veterans thrown out of work as they return to civilian life	
Solution offered by the Truman administration and Congress	

2. Problem: Severe housing shortage	
Solution offered by developers such as William Levitt	
Solutions offered by Congress under the Truman and Eisenhower administrations	

3. Problem: Runaway inflation	
Solution offered by the Truman administration and Congress	

4. Problem: Labor strikes that threaten to cripple the nation	
Solution offered by the Truman administration	

5. Problem: Discrimination and racial violence	
Solutions offered during the Truman administration	

B. On the back of this paper, explain the significance of **suburb, Dixiecrat,** and **Fair Deal.**

CHAPTER 27

Section 2

GUIDED READING *The American Dream in the Fifties*

A. As you read this section, write notes about how Americans were affected by various trends of the 1950s.

Trends	Effects
1. Business expansion: conglomerates and franchises	
2. Suburban expansion: flight from the cities	
3. Population growth: the baby boom	
4. Dramatic increase in leisure time	
5. Dramatic increase in the use of the automobile	
6. The rise of consumerism	

B. On the back of this paper, explain the significance of **suburb, Dixiecrat,** and **Fair Deal.**

Name _____ Date _____

CHAPTER 27

Section 3

GUIDED READING *Popular Culture*

A. As you read this section, take notes to answer questions about innovations and trends in 1950s popular culture.

1. Television	a. What are some of the most popular shows produced?	b. What kinds of subjects did television tend to present?	c. What kinds of subjects did it tend to avoid?
2. Radio	a. How did radio change to compete with television?	b. What role did it play in popularizing African-American culture?	
3. Film	How did movies change to compete with television?		
4. The beat movement	a. Who were the most famous beat writers?	b. What were the movement's chief characteristics?	
5. Rock 'n' roll	a. Who helped to popularize rock 'n' roll?	b. What were rock's chief characteristics?	

B. On the back of this paper, explain the purpose of the **Federal Communications Commission (FCC).**

CHAPTER
27
Section 4

GUIDED READING *The Other America*

A. As you read about problems faced by the "other" America of the 1950s, note some causes of each problem, solutions that were offered, and some effects of those solutions. (Notice that two answers have been provided for you.)

Problem: Decaying Cities		
1. Causes:	Solution offered: *Urban renewal*	2. Effects of solution:

Problem: Discrimination Against Mexican Americans		
Causes: *Prejudice against Hispanics;* *hard feelings toward braceros* *who stayed to work in the* *U.S. after World War II;* *illegal aliens escaping poor* *conditions in Mexico*	3. Solutions offered:	

Problem: Economic Hardship for Native Americans		
4. Causes:	5. Solutions offered:	6. Effects of solutions:

B. On the back of this paper, explain the terms **bracero** and **termination policy.**

Name _____ Date _____

A. As you read this section, complete the time line by taking notes about the election of John F. Kennedy and about his handling of several Soviet-American confrontations.

1957	Launch of *Sputnik 1*	1. What were some of the factors that helped John F. Kennedy win the presidency?
1960	U-2 incident Alignment of Cuba with the Soviet Union U.S. presidential election →	
1961	Bay of Pigs →	2. What were the results of the Bay of Pigs invasion?
	Berlin crisis →	3. How was the Berlin crisis resolved?
1962	Cuban missile crisis →	4. What were the effects of the Cuban missile crisis?
1963	Installation of hot line →	5. Why was the hot line installed?
	Negotiation of Limited Test Ban Treaty →	6. What would the Limited Test Ban Treaty eventually do?

B. On the back of this paper, briefly explain Kennedy's policy of **flexible response.**

Name _____ Date _____

GUIDED READING *The New Frontier*

Section 2

A. As you read this section, take notes to answer questions about President Kennedy's attempts to solve domestic and international problems.

The New Frontier: Fulfilled Promises

Problems	What did Kennedy believe the government could do to solve the problem?	What programs, laws, and accomplishments resulted from Kennedy's beliefs?
1. Economic recession		
2. Poverty abroad		
3. Soviet successes in space		

The New Frontier: Unfulfilled Promises

Rejected Proposals	Later Proposals
4. What reform proposals did Kennedy make that were rejected by a conservative Congress?	5. In 1963, what proposals did Kennedy make but never had the chance to guide through Congress?

Name _____ Date _____

A. As you read, note what each program or law did or was intended to do.

Program or Law	Objectives or Results
1. Tax-cut bill of 1964	
2. Civil Rights Act of 1964	
3. Economic Opportunity Act of 1964	
4. Elementary and Secondary Education Act	
5. Medicare	
6. Medicaid	
7. Immigration Act of 1965	

B. Note how the Court ruled in each case or what the decision accomplished.

Court Cases	Results
1. *Brown* v. *Board of Education*	
2. *Baker* v. *Carr*	
3. *Mapp* v. *Ohio*	
4. *Gideon* v. *Wainright*	
5. *Escobedo* v. *Illinois*	
6. *Miranda* v. *Arizona*	

Name _____ Date _____

CHAPTER
29
Section 1

GUIDED READING *Taking on Segregation*

As you read, answer questions about important events in the civil rights movement.

1875 Civil Rights Act is passed. →	1. What did the Civil Rights Act of 1875 do?
1883 Supreme Court rules 1875 Civil Rights Act unconstitutional.	
1896 *Plessy* v. *Ferguson* →	2. How did the Court rule in *Plessy?*

1945 World War II ends. →	3. In what three ways did World War II help set the stage for the modern civil rights movement? a. b. c.	
1946 *Morgan* v. *Virginia* outlaws mandatory segregation on interstate buses.		
1950 *Sweat* v. *Painter* declares that state law schools must admit black applicants.		
1954 *Brown* v. *Board of Education* →	4. Who argued *Brown's* case?	5. What did the *Brown* ruling declare?
1955 Supreme Court orders school desegregation. Emmett Till is murdered.		
Rosa Parks is arrested. →	6. What organization was formed to support Rosa Parks?	7. What did it do?
1956 Supreme Court outlaws bus segregation.		
1957 Little Rock faces school desegregation crisis. →	8. How did President Eisenhower respond to the Little Rock crisis?	
Southern Christian Leadership Conference (SCLC) is formed. →	9. Who was the president of SCLC?	10. What was SCLC's purpose?
1960 Student Nonviolent Coordination Committee (SNCC) is formed. →	11. What did SNCC accomplish, and how?	

Name _____ Date _____

A. As you read this section, take notes to answer the questions about the time line.

1961	Freedom riders travel → through the South.	1. What was the goal of the freedom riders?	2. What was the Kennedy administration's response?
1962	James Meredith integrates Ole Miss.		
1963	Birmingham and the University of Alabama are integrated.		
	Kennedy sends civil rights bill to Congress.		
	Medgar Evers is murdered.	3. What was the goal of the march on Washington?	4. Who attended the march?
	March on → Washington		
	Birmingham church bombing kills four girls.		
	Kennedy is assassinated.	5. What was the goal of the Freedom Summer project?	6. Who volunteered for the project?
1964	Freedom Summer →		
	Three civil rights workers are murdered.		
	Civil Rights Act is passed.	7. What role did the violence shown on television play in this march?	8. What did the march encourage President Johnson to do?
1965	March from Selma → to Montgomery		
	Voting Rights Act → is passed.	9. What did the Voting Rights Act outlaw?	10. What did the law accomplish?

B. On the back of this paper, explain **Fannie Lou Hamer**'s role in the civil rights movement.

Name _____ Date _____

GUIDED READING *Challenges and Changes*
in the Movement

A. As you read this section, make notes to answer the questions.

1. What is the main difference between de facto and de jure segregation?
2. How did the ideas of SNCC differ from those of the Nation of Islam?
3. How did the early views of Malcolm X differ from his later ideas?
4. What changes took place in Stokely Carmichael's membership in civil rights organizations?
5. How did the ideas of SNCC differ from those of the Black Panthers?

6. What gains were made by the civil rights and Black Power movements? Identify four.

a.	b.	c.	d.

B. On the back of this paper, briefly explain what changes or reforms each of the following called for: **Black Power,** the **Kerner Commission,** and the **Civil Rights Act of 1968.**

Name _____ Date _____

GUIDED READING *Moving Toward Conflict*

Section 1

A. As you read this section, take notes to answer questions about how the United States slowly became involved in a war in Vietnam.

1941	Vietminh is formed. →	1. What did the Vietminh declare as its main goal?
1945	Japan is forced out of Vietnam. →	2. What did Ho Chi Minh declare after Japan was forced out?
1946	French troops return to southern Vietnam. →	3. How did Ho Chi Minh respond to the return of the French?

1950	U.S. begins its involvement in the Vietnam struggle. →	4. Whom did the U.S. support?	5. What aid did the U.S. provide?
		6. Why did the U.S. get involved in the struggle?	
1954	Eisenhower introduces domino theory. →	7. What did Eisenhower compare to a row of dominoes?	
	Vietminh over-runs Dien Bien Phu. →	8. What did this Vietminh victory cause the French to do?	
	Geneva Accords are reached. →	9. How did the Geneva Accords change Vietnam?	
1956	Elections are canceled. →	10. Who canceled the Vietnamese elections? Why?	
1957	Vietcong begins attacks on Diem government.		
1963	Diem is overthrown.	11. What authority did the Tonkin Gulf Resolution grant to the U.S. president?	
1964	U.S. Congress adopts Tonkin Gulf Resolution. →		
1965	Operation - Rolling Thunder is launched. →	12. What did Operation Rolling Thunder do in North Vietnam?	

B. On the back of this paper, explain the importance of the **Ho Chi Minh Trail** in the Vietnam War.

CHAPTER 30

Section 2

GUIDED READING *U.S. Involvement and Escalation*

As you read about the escalation of the war, take notes to answer the questions.

1. What role did each of the following play in the decision to escalate U.S. military involvement in Vietnam?
Lyndon B. Johnson
Robert McNamara
Dean Rusk
William Westmoreland
U.S. Congress
American public opinion

U.S. military strategies result in a bloody stalemate.

2. What military advantages did the Americans have over the Vietcong?	3. What military advantages did the Vietcong have over the Americans?
4. What military strategies did the Americans use against the Vietcong?	5. What military strategies did the Vietcong use against the Americans?

Public support for the war begins to waver as a "credibility gap" grows.

6. What role did each of the following play in this change of public support?
The U.S. economy
Television
The Fulbright hearings

Name _____ Date _____

GUIDED READING *A Nation Divided*

As you read this section, take notes to answer the questions.

Avoiding the War
1. What were some of the ways that young American men avoided military service in Vietnam?
2. In what sense was the Vietnam War a "working-class" war? How did it become one?

Opposing the War
3. What organizations and groups of Americans tended to oppose the war?
4. What were some of the reasons that "doves" opposed the war?
5. In what ways did they show their opposition to the war?

Defending the War
6. By 1967, how did most Americans feel about U.S. involvement in the Vietnam War?
7. Why did "hawks" criticize the Johnson administration's policies in Vietnam?

CHAPTER
30

Section 4

GUIDED READING *1968: A Tumultuous Year*

A. As you read this section, note some of the causes and effects of the events of 1968. Leave the shaded box blank.

Causes	Events of 1968	Effects
	1. Tet Offensive	
	2. Johnson's poor showing in the New Hampshire primary	
	3. Assassination of Dr. Martin Luther King, Jr.	
	4. Assassination of Robert Kennedy	
	5. Disorder at the Democratic National Convention	
	6. Richard M. Nixon's presidential election victory	

B. On the back of this paper, note the political party of each of the following and describe the position that each held or sought in 1968: **Clark Clifford, Eugene McCarthy, Hubert Humphrey,** and **George Wallace.**

Name _____ Date _____

GUIDED READING *The End of the War and Its Legacy*

A. As you read about President Nixon's Vietnam policy and the end of the war, note one or more reasons for each of the following developments during the war.

1. Nixon adopts a policy of Vietnamization.	2. My Lai massacre shocks Americans.
3. Nixon orders invasion of Cambodia.	4. First student strike in U.S. history occurs.
5. Congress repeals the Tonkin Gulf Resolution.	6. The "Christmas bombings" take place.
7. South Vietnam surrenders to North Vietnam.	8. Vietnam veterans receive a cold homecoming.
9. Cambodia erupts in civil war.	10. Congress passes the War Powers Act.
11. The draft is abolished.	12. Many Americans lose faith in their government.

B. On the back of this paper, explain the significance of each of the following terms in relation to the Vietnam War:

silent majority   **Pentagon Papers**   **Henry Kissinger**   **Khmer Rouge**

Name _____ Date _____

CHAPTER
31
Section 1

GUIDED READING *Latinos and Native Americans Seek Equality*

As you read, fill in the chart with answers to the questions.

What did Latinos campaign for?	How did some Latino individuals and groups go about getting what they wanted?	What federal laws (if any) were passed to address these needs?
1. Improved working conditions and better treatment for farm workers		
2. Educational programs for Spanish-speaking students		
3. More political power		

What did Native Americans campaign for?	How did some Native American individuals and groups go about getting what they wanted?	What federal laws (if any) were passed to address these needs?
4. Healthier, more secure lives of their own choosing		
5. Restoration of Indian lands, burial grounds, fishing and timber rights		

An Era of Social Change 121

Name _____ Date _____

A. As you read about the rise of a new women's movement, take notes to explain how each of the following helped to create or advance the movement.

1. Experiences in the workplace	2. Experiences in social activism
3. "Consciousness raising"	4. Feminism
5. Betty Friedan and *The Feminine Mystique*	6. Civil Rights Act of 1964
7. National Organization for Women (NOW)	8. Gloria Steinem and *Ms.* magazine
9. Congress	10. Supreme Court

B. The Equal Rights Amendment would have guaranteed equal rights under the law, regardless of gender. Who opposed this amendment? Why?

1. Who?	2. Why?

Name _____ Date _____

CHAPTER
31

Section 3

GUIDED READING *Culture and Counterculture*

As you read this section, fill out the chart below by listing and describing various elements of the counterculture of the 1960s.

1. Members or participants	2. Beliefs about American society	3. Goals for society and for themselves
4. Movement center	5. Attitudes and activities	6. Violent episodes
7. Impact on art and fashion	8. Impact on music	9. Impact on mainstream America

Name _____ Date _____

CHAPTER 32

Section 1

GUIDED READING *The Nixon Administration*

A. As you read about the Nixon administration, take notes to describe President
Nixon's policies toward the problems facing him.

Problems	Policies
1. Size and power of the federal government	
2. Inefficiency of the welfare system	
3. Vietnam War and domestic disorder	
4. Nixon's reelection	
5. Liberalism of Supreme Court justices	
6. Stagflation and recession	
7. U.S.–China relations	
8. U.S.–Soviet relations	

B. On the back of this paper, explain the significance of **realpolitik** and **OPEC**
during the Nixon years.

Name _____ Date _____

GUIDED READING *Watergate: Nixon's Downfall*

Section 2

As you read about Watergate, answer the questions shown on the following time line.

1972

June — Break-in at DNC campaign office

→ 1. How were the "plumbers" connected to President Nixon?

Nov. — Nixon wins reelection.

1973

Jan. — Plumbers go on trial.

→ 2. Who was the judge? Why did he hand out maximum sentences?

Mar. — Mitchell and Dean are implicated.

→ 3. How were Mitchell and Dean connected to Nixon?

April — Dean is fired; Haldeman and Erlichman resign.

→ 4. How were Haldeman and Erlichman connected to Nixon?

May — Senate opens Watergate hearings.

→ 5. What did the following men tell the Senate about Nixon?

  a. Dean

  b. Butterfield

Oct. — Saturday Night Massacre

→ 6. Who was fired or forced to resign in the "massacre"?

1974

April — Edited transcripts of tapes are released.

→ 7. Why weren't investigators satisfied with the transcripts?

July — Supreme Court orders surrender of tapes.

Aug. — House committee adopts impeachment articles.

Unedited tapes are released.

→ 8. What did the tapes reveal?

Nixon resigns.

Name _____ Date _____

A. As you read about Presidents Ford and Carter, take notes to describe the policies
of each toward the problems facing them.

Problems Faced by Ford	Policies
1. Ending Watergate scandal	
2. Troubled economy	
3. Hostile Congress	
4. Cold War tensions	
5. Southeast Asia	

Problems Faced by Carter	Policies
6. Distrust of politicians	
7. Energy crisis	
8. Discrimination	
9. Human rights issues	
10. Panama Canal	
11. Cold War tensions	
12. Middle East tensions	

B. On the back of this paper, explain the importance of the **Camp David Accords**
and the **Ayatollah Ruhollah Khomeini** to the Carter administration.

Name _____ Date _____

CHAPTER
32
Section 4

GUIDED READING *Environmental Activism*

A. As you read about the nation's efforts to address environmental problems, take notes to describe how American attitudes were affected by each event or how the event affected the environment itself.

Events	Effects on Attitudes or Environment
1. Publication of Rachel Carson's *Silent Spring* →	
2. Celebration of Earth Day →	
3. Creation of the Environmental Protection Agency →	
4. Passage of the new Clean Air Act →	
5. Passage of the Alaska Native Claims Settlement Act →	
6. Nuclear accident at Three Mile Island →	

B. On the back of this paper, define **environmentalist.**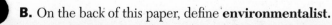

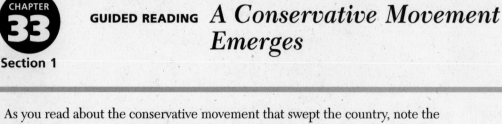

GUIDED READING *A Conservative Movement Emerges*

CHAPTER **33**
Section 1

A. As you read about the conservative movement that swept the country, note the individuals, groups, and institutions that fueled it. Then identify issues the New Right emphasized as well as the interests it promoted.

1. Individuals	2. Groups and institutions

3. Issues and interests

B. Identify four factors that contributed to Ronald Reagan's victory.

1.	3.
2.	4.

C. On the back of this paper, define **entitlement program** and **reverse discrimination.**

Name _____ Date _____

CHAPTER 33
Section 2

GUIDED READING *Conservative Policies Under Reagan and Bush*

A. As you read, note the results of "Reaganomics" and of actions taken to achieve important goals of the conservative movement.

Goal: Stimulate the economy
1. Cut government spending on social programs and lowered income taxes   →   Result(s):
2. Increased military spending   →   Result(s):

Goal: Promote traditional values and morality
3. Named conservative judges to the Supreme Court and other federal courts   →   Result(s):

Goal: Reduce the size and power of the federal government
5. Cut the Environmental Protection Agency budget and appointed EPA administrators sympathetic to business   →   Result(s):

B. On the back of this paper, define **supply-side economics.** Then identify **Sandra Day O'Connor**, **William Rehnquist**, and **Geraldine Ferraro.**

The Conservative Tide 129

CHAPTER
33
Section 3

GUIDED READING *Social Concerns in the 1980s*

A. As you read, identify specific issues in each of the following areas that concerned
Americans in the 1980s.

1. Health	2. Education	3. Cities

B. Take notes about the gains, losses, and chief concerns of each of the following groups.

1. Women	2. African Americans	3. Latinos
4. Native Americans	5. Asian Americans	6. Gays and lesbians

C. On the back of this paper, note what **L. Douglas Wilder** and **Jesse Jackson** did
to advance African Americans politically.

CHAPTER
33
Section 4

GUIDED READING *Foreign Policy After the Cold War*

As you read about the end of the Cold War, note key persons, events, and trends involved in the nations listed below. Concentrate on political and economic developments as well as on U.S. relations with those countries. Leave the shaded boxes blank.

Nations	Key Individuals	Key Events and Trends
1. Soviet Union		Events: Trends:
2. Poland		Events: Trends:
3. Germany		Events: Trends:
4. Yugoslavia		Events: Trends:
5. China		Events: Trends:
6. Nicaragua		Events: Trends:
7. Panama		Events: Trends:
8. Iran		
9. Iraq		

GUIDED READING *The 1990s and the*
New Millennium

A. As you read, write notes in the appropriate boxes to answer the questions.

The 1992 Presidential Elections		
1. a. Who ran as a Republican?	2. a. Who ran as an independent?	3. a. Who ran as a Democrat?
b. Why did he fail to convince voters to support him?	b. What created an opportunity for this independent candidacy?	b. What helped him win?

The Clinton Administration's First Term	
4. What did Clinton achieve in domestic policy?	5. What did Clinton achieve in foreign policy?

The Republican Congress and the Contract with America	
6. What goals did the contract set for Republican leaders?	7. How did Clinton and the Senate undermine the contract?

B. On the back of this paper, identify **Hillary Rodham Clinton** and **Newt Gingrich** and briefly describe one success and one failure each experienced during Clinton's first term.

Name _____ Date _____

CHAPTER 34

Section 2

GUIDED READING *The New Global Economy*

A. As you read this section, take notes to answer questions about the U.S. role in the changing world economy.

The Domestic Economy: Good News and Bad News	
1. What was the good news?	2. What was the bad news?

The Changing Domestic Economy	
3. What trends led to explosive growth in the service sector? How were workers affected?	
4. What trends led to explosive growth in temporary work? How were workers affected?	
5. What trends led to a sharp decline in manufacturing jobs? How were workers affected?	
6. What trends led to explosive growth in the high-tech industry? How were workers affected?	

The Changing Global Economy	
7. What trends affected international trade and competition? How did those trends affect U.S. businesses and workers?	

B. On the back of this paper, explain why **Bill Gates** is a significant figure. Then tell what **GATT** stands for and what it did.

CHAPTER
34
Section 3

GUIDED READING *Technology and Modern Life*

A. As you read about the impact of technological advances during the 1990s, note inventions, trends, and efforts relating to each field listed below.

1. Communications
2. Health care
3. Genetic engineering
4. Entertainment
5. Education
6. Space exploration
7. Environment

B. On the back of this paper, explain the significance of the **Telecommunications Act of 1996.**

CHAPTER
34
Section 4

GUIDED READING *The Changing Face of America*

A. As you read this section, note three facts or statistics concerning each of the following important trends in the late 20th century.

URBAN FLIGHT	1. 2. 3.
BABY BOOMERS	4. 5. 6.
IMMIGRATION	7. 8. 9.

B. Note one challenge the United States will face in each of the following areas during the 21st century.

1. Urban and Suburban Life	
2. Aging Population	
3. Immigration Policy	

C. On the back of this paper, define **telecommute**.